Our Debt to Greece and Rome

EDITORS

GEORGE DEPUE HADZSITS, PH.D.

University of Pennsylvania

DAVID MOORE ROBINSON, PH.D., LL.D.

The Johns Hopkins University

CONTRIBUTORS TO THE "OUR DEBT TO
GREECE AND ROME FUND," WHOSE
GENEROSITY HAS MADE POSSIBLE
THE LIBRARY

Our Debt to Greece and Rome

Philadelphia
DR. ASTLEY P. C. ASHHURST
JOHN C. BELL
HENRY H. BONNELL
JASPER YEATES BRINTON
GEORGE BURNHAM, JR.
JOHN CADWALADER
MISS CLARA COMEGYS
MISS MARY E. CONVERSE
ARTHUR G. DICKSON
WILLIAM M. ELKINS
H. H. FURNESS, JR.
WILLIAM P. GEST
JOHN GRIBBEL
SAMUEL F. HOUSTON
CHARLES EDWARD INGERSOLL
JOHN STORY JENKS
ALBA B. JOHNSON
MISS NINA LEA
GEORGE MCFADDEN
MRS. JOHN MARKOE
JULES E. MASTBAUM
J. VAUGHAN MERRICK
EFFINGHAM B. MORRIS
WILLIAM R. MURPHY
JOHN S. NEWBOLD
S. DAVIS PAGE (*memorial*)
OWEN J. ROBERTS
JOSEPH G. ROSENGARTEN
WILLIAM C. SPROUL
JOHN B. STETSON, JR.
DR. J. WILLIAM WHITE
  (*memorial*)
GEORGE D. WIDENER
MRS. JAMES D. WINSOR
OWEN WISTER
  The Philadelphia Society
for the Promotion of Liberal
Studies.

Boston
ORIC BATES (*memorial*)
FREDERICK P. FISH
WILLIAM AMORY GARDNER
JOSEPH CLARK HOPPIN

Chicago
HERBERT W. WOLFF

Cincinnati
CHARLES PHELPS TAFT

Cleveland
SAMUEL MATHER

Detroit
JOHN W. ANDERSON
DEXTER M. FERRY, JR.

Doylestown, Pennsylvania
"A LOVER OF GREECE AND
  ROME"

New York
JOHN JAY CHAPMAN
WILLARD V. KING
THOMAS W. LAMONT
DWIGHT W. MORROW
MRS. D. W. MORROW
ELIHU ROOT
MORTIMER L. SCHIFF
WILLIAM SLOANE
GEORGE W. WICKERSHAM
And one contributor, who
  has asked to have his name
  withheld:
*Maecenas atavis edite regibus,
O et praesidium et dulce decus
meum.*

Washington
  The Greek Embassy at
Washington, for the Greek
Government.

[ii]

The following lovers of Greek literature, and of Sappho in particular, have kindly consented to act as patrons and have made possible, by generous contributions, the larger size of this volume in the Series "Our Debt to Greece and Rome":

PLATE I. ALMA TADEMA'S SAPPHO
In the Walters' Art Gallery, Baltimore

SAPPHO
AND HER INFLUENCE

BY

DAVID M. ROBINSON, Ph.D., LL.D.

*W. H. Collins Vickers Professor of Archaeology and
Epigraphy and Lecturer on Greek Literature
The Johns Hopkins University*

MARSHALL JONES COMPANY
BOSTON · MASSACHUSETTS

To

THE MEMORY OF

BASIL LANNEAU GILDERSLEEVE

MASTER, COLLEAGUE, AND FRIEND

AND TO MY FORMER TEACHERS

EDWARD CAPPS

PAUL SHOREY

ULRICH VON WILAMOWITZ-MOELLENDORFF

δῶρον ᾿αντὶ μεγάλου σμικρόν
A trifling gift in return for much.

Ἕτερος ἐξ ἐτέρου σοφὸς τό τε πάλαι τό τε νῦν.
οὐδὲ γὰρ ῥᾷστον ἀρρήτων ἐπέων πύλας
ἐξευρεῖν.

Poet is heir to poet, now as of yore; for in
sooth 'tis no light task to find the gates of
virgin song.

JEBB, *Bacchylides*, p. 413, frag. 4

Immortal *Sappho, maid divine,*
Thou sharest with the heavenly nine
All honor.   Shout through all the town
That on her head we place a crown.
Hasten with the chaplet green,
Greet her one and all as queen;
The Lesbian, a tenth muse we name,
And prophesy that her bright fame
Shall spread o'er all the world.
This title till the stars do fall,
Nations yet unborn shall call
And glorify her name.

(LUCY MILBURN)

CONTENTS

CONTENTS

ILLUSTRATIONS

ILLUSTRATIONS

SAPPHO
AND HER INFLUENCE

SAPPHO AND HER INFLUENCE

I. SOME APPRECIATIONS, ANCIENT AND MODERN

THE NAME of Sappho will never die. But it lives in most of the minds that know it at all to-day as hardly more than the hazy nucleus of a ragged fringe suggestive of erotic thoughts or of sexual perversion. Very seldom does it evoke the vision of a great and pure poetess with marvellous expressions of beauty, grace, and power at her command, who not only haunts the dawn of Grecian Lyric poetry but lives in scattered and broken lights that glint from vases and papyri and from the pages of cold grammarians and warm admirers, whose eulogies we would gladly trade for the unrecorded poems which they quote so meagerly. Sappho has furnished the title of such a novel as Daudet's *Sapho*. It figures in suggestive moving pictures.[1] The name will answer prettily as that of a bird or even a boat such as the yacht with which Mr. Douglas defended the American cup in 1871. The modern idea of Sappho truly seems to be based mainly on Daudet, who with Pierre Louys in recent times has done most to degrade her good character and who goes so far as to say that "the word Sappho itself by the force of rolling descent through ages is encrusted with unclean legends and has degenerated from the name of a goddess to that of a malady." But to the lover of lyrics, who is also a student of Greek Literature in Greek, this poetess of passion becomes a living and illustrious personality, who of all the poets of the world, as Symonds says, is the "one whose every word has a peculiar and unmistakable perfume, a seal of absolute perfection and inimitable grace." "Sappho," says Tennyson in *The Princess*, "in arts of grace vied with any man." She is one whose fervid fragments, as the great Irish translator of the *Odes* of Anacreon and the *Anacreontics*, Thomas Moore, says in his *Evenings in Greece*,

> *Still, like sparkles of Greek Fire,*
> *Undying, even beneath the wave,*
> *Burn on thro' time and ne'er expire,*

[4]

a prophecy still true even in this material-
istic day. Sappho, herself, had intimations
of immortality, for she writes with perfect
beauty and modesty:

> Μνάσεσθαί τινά φαμι καὶ ὕστερον ἀμμέων
> I *say some one will think of us hereafter.*

This brief, pellucid verse Swinburne in his
Anactoria has distorted into the gorgeous emotional rhetoric of fourteen verses. But its own
quiet prophecy stands good to-day. A fragment first published in 1922 [2] also seems to
make her say:

> *and yet great*
> *glory will come to thee in all places*
> *where Phaëthon* [*shines*]
> *and even in Acheron's halls*
> [*thou shalt be honored.*]

In general, antiquity thought of her as "*the*
poetess" κατ'ἐξοχήν, ἡ ποιήτρια,[3] just as Professor
Harmon has recently shown [4] that "the poet"
in ancient literature means Homer. Down to
the present day Sappho has kept the definite
article which antiquity gave her and has been
called *the* poetess, though we must be careful to
test a writer's use of the term. Therefore, we

[5]

must not understand by the absence of any
added epithet, as Wharton does, that Tennyson
rates her higher than all other poets, merely
because in *Locksley Hall, Sixty Years After* he
speaks of Sappho as "The Poet," having called
her in his youth "The Ancient Poetess," [5] —
for he also speaks of Dante as "The Poet,"
when in *Locksley Hall* he says, "this is truth
the poet sings," and then cites verse 121 of the
Inferno. It is rare, however, even in modern
times to find Sappho classed with any other
poet as a peer, as in the beautiful tribute *To
Christina Rossetti* of William Watson, one of
the best modern writers of epigrams, where
Mrs. Browning and Sappho are the two other
women referred to:

> *Songstress, in all times ended and begun,*
> *Thy billowy-bosom'd fellows are not three.*
> *Of those sweet peers, the grass is green o'er one;*
> *And blue above the other is the sea.*

In ancient days Pinytus (1st cent. A.D.) composed this epigram: [6]

> *This tomb reveals where Sappho's ashes lie,*
> *But her sweet words of wisdom ne'er will die.*
> (LORD NAEVES)

[6]

Tullius Laureas, who wrote both in Greek and Latin about 60 B.C., puts into her mouth the following: "When you pass my Aeolian grave, stranger, call not the songstress of Mytilene dead. For 'tis true this tomb was built by the hands of men, and such works of humankind sink swiftly into oblivion; yet if you ask after me for the sake of the holy Muses from each of whom I have taken a flower for my posy of nine, you shall know that I have escaped the darkness of Death, and no sun shall ever rise that keepeth not the name of the lyrist Sappho." (Edmonds, with variations.)

Posidippus [7] (250 B.C.) says:

> *Sappho's white, speaking pages of dear song*
> *Yet linger with us and will linger long.*

> (T. DAVIDSON)

Horace [8] says:

> *vivuntque commissi calores*
> *Aeoliae fidibus puellae.*

That inadequate and misleading metaphor of fire, as Mackail says, recurs in all her eulogists. Μεμιγμένα πυρὶ φθέγγεται, "her words are mingled with fire," writes Plutarch,[9] but the "fire" of the burning Sappho is not raging hot, it is an unscorching calm, brilliant lustre that

[7]

makes other poetry seem cold by comparison. No wonder that Hermesianax [10] (about 290 B.C.) called her "that nightingale of hymns" and Lucian [11] "the honeyed boast of the Lesbians." Strabo (i A.D.) said: "Sappho is a marvellous creature (θαυμαστόν τι χρῆμα), in all history you will find no woman who can challenge comparison with her even in the slightest degree." Antipater of Thessalonica (10 B.C.) named Sappho as one of the nine poetesses who were god-tongued and called her one of the nine muses: "The female Homer: Sappho pride and choice of Lesbian dames, whose locks have earned a name." [12] In another epigram in the *Anthology*, [13] probably from the base of a lost statue of Sappho in the famous library at Pergamum, [14] and which Jucundus and Cyriac were able to cite many hundreds of years later, Antipater says,

> *Sappho my name, in song o'er women held*
> *As far supreme as Homer men excelled.*

> (NEAVES)

> *Some thoughtlessly proclaim the muses nine;*
> *A tenth is Lesbian Sappho, maid divine,*

are the words of Plato in Lord Neaves' translation of an epigram of which Wilamowitz [15] now

[8]

timidly defends the genuineness. Antipater of
Sidon (150 B.C.) [16] in his encomium on Sappho
tells how

> *Amazement seized Mnemosyne*
> *At Sappho's honey'd song:*
> *'What, does a tenth muse,' then, cried she,*
> *'To mortal men belong!'*
>
> (WELLESLEY)

He also speaks [17] of Sappho as "one that is
sung for a mortal Muse among Muses immortal
. . . a delight unto Greece." Dioscorides [18]
(180 B.C.) says: "Sappho, thou Muse of Aeolian
Eresus, sweetest of all love-pillows unto the
burning young, sure am I that Pieria or ivied
Helicon must honour thee, along with the
Muses, seeing that thy spirit is their spirit."
Again, in an anonymous epigram [19] it is said:
"her song will seem Calliope's own voice."
Another writer, [20] also anonymous, discussing
the nine lyric poets, says:

> *Sappho would make a ninth; but fitter she*
> *Among the Muses, a tenth Muse to be.*
>
> (NEAVES)

Catullus [21] speaks of the *Sapphica Musa*, and
Ausonius in Epigram XXXII calls her *Lesbia
Pieriis Sappho soror addita Musis.*[22]

If we turn now from the praise of the an-

cients to modern literary critics of classic lore
we shall not find any depreciation but rather
an enhancing of that ancient praise. The classic
estimate of Sappho holds its own and more
than holds it to-day. J. A. K. Thomson in his
Greeks and Barbarians [23] says: "Landor is not
Greek any more than Leconte de Lisle is Greek.
. . . they have not the banked and inward-
burning fire which makes Sappho so different."
Mackail speaks of "the feeling expressed in
splendid but hardly exaggerated language by
Swinburne, in that early poem where, alone
among the moderns, he has mastered and all
but reproduced one of her favourite metres, the
Sapphic stanza which she invented and to which
she gave her name" —

Ah the singing, ah the delight, the passion!
All the Loves wept, listening; sick with anguish,
Stood the crowned nine Muses about Apollo;
　　　Fear was upon them,

While the tenth sang wonderful things they knew not.
Ah, the tenth, the Lesbian! the nine were silent,
None endured the sound of her song for weeping;
　　　Laurel by laurel,

Faded all their crowns; but about her forehead
　　. . . . .
Shone a light of fire as a crown for ever.

Swinburne himself was thoroughly steeped in Sappho whom he considered "the supreme success, the final achievement of the poetic art." He laid abounding tribute at her feet both in verse and prose. In an appreciation first published posthumously in 1914 in *The Living Age*,[24] he says: "Judging even from the mutilated fragments fallen within our reach from the broken altar of her sacrifice of song, I for one have always agreed with all Grecian tradition in thinking Sappho to be beyond all question and comparison *the very greatest poet that ever lived.* Aeschylus is the greatest poet who ever was also a prophet; Shakespeare is the greatest dramatist who ever was also a poet, but Sappho is simply nothing less — as she is certainly nothing more — than the greatest poet who ever was at all. Such at least is the simple and sincere profession of my lifelong faith." Alfred Noyes recognizes in Swinburne's praise of Sappho a spirit which would make them congenial companions in another world, when in the poem *In Memory of Swinburne* he writes:

THEE, *the storm-bird, nightingale-souled,*
　　Brother of Sappho, the seas reclaim!
Age upon age have the great waves rolled
　　Mad with her music, exultant, aflame;

[11]

Thee, thee too, shall their glory enfold,
Lit with thy snow-winged fame.

Back, thro' the years, fleets the sea-bird's wing:
Sappho, of old time, once, — *ah, hark!*
So did he love her of old and sing!
Listen, he flies to her, back thro' the dark!
Sappho, of old time, once . . . *Yea, Spring*
Calls him home to her, hark!

Sappho, long since, in the years far sped,
Sappho, I loved thee! *Did I not seem*
Fosterling only of earth? I have fled,
Fled to thee, sister. Time is a dream!
Shelley is here with us! Death lies dead!
Ah, how the bright waves gleam.

Wide was the cage-door, idly swinging;
April touched me and whispered 'Come.'
Out and away to the great deep winging,
Sister, I flashed to thee over the foam,
Out to the sea of Eternity, singing
'Mother, thy child comes home.'

J. W. Mackail echoes Swinburne's high
praise: "Many women have written poetry
and some have written poetry of high merit
and extreme beauty. But no other woman can
claim an assured place in the first rank of
poets" . . . . "The sole woman of any age or

country who gained and still holds an unchallenged place in the first rank of the world's poets, she is also one of the few poets of whom it may be said with confidence that they hold of none and borrow of none, and that their poetry is, in some unique way, an immediate inspiration."

Many another modern critic ranks Sappho as supreme. Typical are such eulogies as "Sappho, the most famous of all women" (Aldington), or "Sappho, incomparably the greatest poetess the world has ever seen" (Watts-Dunton in ninth ed. *Encyclopædia Britannica*).

II. SAPPHO'S LIFE, LESBUS, HER LOVE–AFFAIRS, HER PERSONALITY AND PUPILS

IT IS my purpose in the limited space at my disposal to show in a general way, since it will not be possible to go into details, the truth of Sappho's prophecy that men would think of her [25] in after-times: to show her importance as a woman and poetess and our debt to her, and also to give my readers some acquaintance with the real and the unreal Sappho so that they can judge how much is fact and how much is fancy in what they hear and read about Sappho, thus proving again that the warp and woof of literature cannot be understood without a knowledge of the original Greek threads. This chapter will consider Sappho's Life.

Unfortunately we know little of Sappho herself, and about that little there is doubt. Even the ancient lives of Sappho are lost. If we had Chamaeleon's work on Sappho,[26] or the exegesis of Sappho and Alcaeus [27] by Callias of Mytilene, or the book on Sappho's metres by Dracon of Stratonicea, we should not be left so in the dark;

but all these have perished or, what comes to the same thing, are undiscovered. Like Homer, Sappho gives us almost no definite information about herself, and we must depend on late lexicographers, commentators, and imitators. Villainous stories arose about her and gathered added vileness till they reached a climax in the licentious Latin of Ovid, especially as seen in Pope's translation of the epistle of Sappho to Phaon.

Sappho came of a noble family belonging to an Aeolian colony in the Troad. Though Suidas gives eight possibilities for the name of Sappho's father, the most probable is Scamandronymus, a good Asia Minor name vouched for by Herodotus, Aelian and other ancient writers and now confirmed by a recently discovered papyrus.[28] He was rich and noble and probably a wine-merchant. He died, according to Ovid,[29] when Sappho's eldest child was six years of age.

Her mother's name, says Suidas, was Cleïs.[30] Commentators assume that she was living when Sappho began to write poetry because of the reference to "mother" in the "Spinner in Love"; but this may be an impersonal poem. According to the Greek custom of naming the child after a grandparent the poetess called her only daughter Cleïs.

[15]

The poetess had three brothers, Charaxus, Larichus, who held the aristocratic office of cup-bearer in the Prytaneum to the highest officials of Mytilene, and, according to Suidas, a third brother, Eurygyius,[31] of whom nothing is known.

Athenaeus tells us that the beautiful Sappho often sang the praises of her brother Larichus; and the name was handed down in families of Mytilene, for it occurs in a Priene inscription [32] as the name of the father of a friend of Alexander who was named Eurygyius. This shows the family tradition and how descendants of Sappho's family attained high ranks in Alexander's army.

Charaxus, the eldest brother as we now know, "sailed to Egypt and as an associate with a certain Doricha spent very much money on her," according to the recently found late papyrus biography. Charaxus had strayed from home about 572 and sailed as a merchant to Naucratis, the great Greek port colony established in the delta of the Nile under conditions similar to those of China's treaty-ports. There he was bartering Lesbian wine, Horace's *innocentis pocula Lesbii*, for loveliness and pleasures, when he fell in love with and ransomed the beautiful Thracian courtesan, the world-renowned *demi-mondaine*. She was called Doricha

[16]

by Sappho according to the Augustan geographer, Strabo, but Herodotus names her Rhodopis, rosy-cheeked,[33] and evidently thought she had contributed to Delphi [34] the collection of *obeliskoi* or iron spits, the small change of ancient days before coin money was used to any great extent. Herodotus, the only writer preserved before 400 B.C. who gives us any details about Sappho tells the story and how the sister roundly rebuked her brother in a poem. Some four hundred years later Strabo, adding a legend which recalls that of Cinderella, repeats the story and it is retold by Athenaeus after another two hundred years. In our own day it has slightly influenced William Morris in the *Earthly Paradise*. Except for archaeology, however, we should never have heard Sappho's own words. About 1898 the sands of Egypt gave up five mutilated stanzas of this poem which scholars had for many a year longed to hear, but the beginnings of the lines are gone and only a few letters of the last stanza remain. My own interest in Sappho dates from that very year when I wrote for Professor Edward Capps, then of the University of Chicago, a detailed seminary paper on *The Nereid Ode*, and for the twenty-five years since I have been gathering

[17]

material about Sappho. We must be careful
not to accept as certainly Sappho's, especially
the un-Sapphic idea of the last stanza, the
restorations of Wilamowitz, Edmonds, and a
host of other scholars, who have changed their
own conjectures several times. Wilamowitz
goes so far as to think that the words apply to
Larichus, but most critics have restored them
with reference to Charaxus. I give a version
which I have based on Edmonds' latest and
revised text,[35] taking a model from the stanza
used by Tennyson in his *Palace of Art*.

In offering a new translation of such songs
as these it should be fully realized that no
translation of a really beautiful poem can possibly represent the original in any fair or complete fashion. Unfortunately languages differ;
and in translating a single word of Sappho into
a word of English which fairly represents its
meaning, one may easily have lost the musical
charm of the original, and still further he may
have broken up the general charm or spirit
which the word has because of its associations
with the spirit of the whole song. It ought to
be clear that in preserving the literal meanings
of the words in a song the translator may be
compelled to part in large measure with the

musical note that comes from assonance, alliteration, and association; or again that in rendering the music as Swinburne could do, he may
have diluted or even lost the real meaning and
spirit of the poem; and finally that, though the
spirit of the poem may be seized ever so effec-
tively, the working out of the details of music
and meaning may fail to respond to those of
the original. Of course a slight measure of
successful representation may be attained. But
whatever poetical value anyone senses in these
translations must be almost indefinitely height-
ened by imagination, if the beauty, grace, and
power of the original are to be realized. Why
then translate at all? Well, just because of a
desire to make an English reader share even in
a small measure the pleasure the translator feels
in the original and to furnish him with paths
along which his imagination may lawfully climb
toward the height reached by this strangely
gifted woman's pen.

TO THE NEREIDS

O ALL *ye Nereids crowned with golden hair*
  My brother bring, back home, I pray.
His heart's true wish both good and fair
  Accomplished, every way.

[19]

May *he for former errors make amend —*
  If once to sin his feet did go —
Become *a joy, again, to every friend,*
  A grief to every foe.

O *may our house through no man come to shame,*
  O may he now be glad to bring
Some *share of honor to his sister's name.*
  Her heart with joy will sing.

Some *bitter words there were that passed his lip, —*
  For me the wrath of love made fierce
And *him resentful, — just as he took ship,*
  When to the quick did pierce

My *song-shaft sharp.   He sought to crush my*
    heart, —
  Not distant be the feasting day
When *civic welcome on his fellows' part,*
  Shall laugh all wrath away!

And *may a wife, if he desires, be found*
  In wedlock due, with worthy rite —
But *as for thee, thou black-skinned female hound,*
  Baleful and evil sprite,

Set *to the ground thy low malodorous snout*
  And let my brother go his way
Whilst *thou, along thy low-lived paths, track out*
  The trail of meaner prey.

                                    (D. M. R.)

In this letter, handed perhaps to Charaxus
on his return from Egypt, the tone is that of

reconciliation rather than that of rebuke, and
the rebuke itself may be found in a fragment
of another letter, if Edmonds' restoration is
anywhere near the truth.[35]

> *You seek the false and shun the true,*
> *And bid your friends go hang for you,*
> *And grieve me in your pride and say*
> *I bring you shame. Go, have your way,*
> *And flaunt me till you've had your fill;*
> *I have no fears and never will*
> *For the anger of a child.*
>
> (EDMONDS)

"Sappho," or "Sapho,"[36] as the name appears
on vases and papyri, or "Psappho," as coins
and vases have it, or "Psappha," as she herself
spelled it in her soft Aeolic dialect, is perhaps
a nom de plume, — the word meaning *lapis laz-
uli*. According to Athenaeus [37] (who wrote at
the beginning of the third century A.D.) she
lived in the time of the father of Croesus, Alyat-
tes, who reigned over Lydia from 628 to 560 B.C.
Jeremiah, Nebuchadnezzar, and at Rome Tar-
quinius Priscus were her contemporaries. Suidas, a Greek lexicographer of the tenth century
A.D., says that she flourished about the 42nd
Olympiad (612–608 B.C.),[38] along with Alcaeus and
Stesichorus and Pittacus,[39] (Pl. 2) the latter, one

[21]

of the seven wise men of Greece and lord of Lesbus. This would indicate that she was then in her poetic prime. If so, she must have been born about 630 B.C. or earlier. Mackail dates her birth as far back as the middle of the seventh century. These early dates given above are amply confirmed by her explicit reference to Sardis and by her descriptions of the luxurious life of the Lydians (E.[40] 20, 38, 86, 130, etc.) which have lately been made so realistic by the American excavations with their finds of gold staters of Croesus, beautiful Lydian seals, jewelry, pottery, and inscriptions.

In the seventh century after the founding of Naucratis, about 650 B.C., many Mytilenaeans migrated to Naucratis and engaged in trade in wine and other products.[41] Among these was included, as Herodotus' story shows, Sappho's brother Charaxus; the mention of his name furnishes a further confirmation of the date we have assumed, and proves that Sappho lived at least after 572 B.C., the year of the accession to the throne of Egypt of Amasis, in whose reign Herodotus [42] says that Rhodopis flourished. This would make Sappho's age at the time about sixty and justify the epithet of "old" which she applies to herself in the poem given in

[22]

Edmonds 99. Fragment 42 in Edmonds seems to
say " age now causeth a thousand twisted wrin-
kles to make their track along my face." [43] Stobaeus [44] tells how one evening over the wine
Solon's nephew, Execestides, sang to him a song
by Sappho, and Solon requested him to teach it
to him that he might learn it before he died.
Now Solon was one of the seven to whom
Pittacus also belonged. He died about 559 B.C.
at the age of eighty, and the incident serves to
indicate that Sappho's poems were coming into
vogue among the young Athenians in Solon's
old age.

Sappho's birthplace was Eresus,[45] the birthplace also of Aristotle's famous pupil Theophrastus. She early moved to Mytilene (Pl. 3),
chief city of Lesbus. Lesbus had been renowned
for lovely ladies from Homer's day, when beauty
contests were held there, as they have been
down to the present time. It had also been
famous from early days for its sweet wine.
Many an ancient author speaks of this whole-
some tipple, and to-day a thirsty traveller is
delighted to sit in a café on the quay and drink
a glass of the fine modern κρασὶ τῆς Μιτυλήνης.

Lesbus was so near to Lydia that it could not
help absorbing some of the Ionian and Lydian

luxury. No one has better described the position of Lesbus in Greek literature than Symonds:[46]

"For a certain space of time the Aeolians occupied the very foreground of Greek literature, and blazed out with a brilliance of lyrical splendor that has never been surpassed. There seems to have been something passionate and intense in their temperament, which made the emotions of the Dorian and the Ionian feeble by comparison. Lesbos, the centre of Aeolian culture, was the island of overmastering passions: the personality of the Greek race burned there with a fierce and steady flame of concentrated feeling. The energies which the Ionians divided between pleasure, politics, trade, legislation, science, and the arts, and which the Dorians turned to war and statecraft and social economy, were restrained by the Aeolians within the sphere of individual emotions, ready to burst forth volcanically. Nowhere in any age of Greek history, or in any part of Hellas, did the love of physical beauty, the sensibility to radiant scenes of nature, the consuming fervor of personal feeling, assume such grand proportions and receive so illustrious an expression as they did in Lesbos. At first this passion blossomed into the most exquisite lyrical poetry that the world has known; this was the flower-time of the Aeolians, their brief and brilliant spring. But the fruit it bore was bitter and rotten. Lesbos became a byword for corruption. The passions which for a moment had flamed into the gorgeousness of art, burning their envelope of words and images, remained a mere furnace of sensuality, from which no expression of the divine

[24]

in human life could be expected. In this the Lesbian poets were not unlike the Provençal troubadours, who made a literature of love, or the Venetian painters, who based their art upon the beauty of color, the voluptuous charms of the flesh. In each case the motive of enthusiastic passion sufficed to produce a dazzling result. But as soon as its freshness was exhausted there was nothing left for art to live on, and mere decadence to sensuality ensued."

"Several circumstances contributed to aid the development of lyric poetry in Lesbos. The customs of the Aeolians permitted more social and domestic freedom than was common in Greece. Aeolian women were not confined to the harem like Ionians, or subjected to the rigorous discipline of the Spartans. While mixing freely with male society, they were highly educated, and accustomed to express their sentiments to an extent unknown elsewhere in history — until, indeed, the present time. The Lesbian ladies applied themselves successfully to literature. They formed clubs for the cultivation of poetry and music. They studied the arts of beauty, and sought to refine metrical forms and diction. Nor did they confine themselves to the scientific side of art. Unrestrained by public opinion, and passionate for the beautiful, they cultivated their senses and emotions, and indulged their wildest passions. All the luxuries and elegancies of life which that climate and the rich valleys of Lesbos could afford were at their disposal; exquisite gardens, where the rose and hyacinth spread perfume; river-beds ablaze with the oleander and wild pomegranate; olive-groves and fountains, where the cyclamen and violet flowered with feathery maiden-hair; pinetree-shadowed coves,

[25]

where they might bathe in the calm of a tideless sea; fruits such as only the southern sun and sea-wind can mature; marble cliffs, starred with jonquil and anemone in spring, aromatic with myrtle and lentisk and samphire and wild rosemary through all the months; nightingales that sang in May; temples dim with dusky gold and bright with ivory; statues and frescoes of heroic forms. In such scenes as these the Lesbian poets lived, and thought of love. When we read their poems, we seem to have the perfumes, colors, sounds, and lights of that luxurious land distilled in verse. Nor was a brief but biting winter wanting to give tone to their nerves, and, by contrast with the summer, to prevent the palling of so much luxury on sated senses. The voluptuousness of Aeolian poetry is not like that of Persian or Arabian art. It is Greek in its self-restraint, proportion, tact. We find nothing burdensome in its sweetness. All is so rhythmically and sublimely ordered in the poems of Sappho that supreme art lends solemnity and grandeur to the expression of unmitigated passion."

A young woman of good birth in such surroundings would be sure to have her love-affairs. When Sappho was at the height of her fame in young womanhood, the poet Alcaeus, her townsman, was also in his glory. We are not told whether he was older or younger than she, but probably Sappho was the older and lived before the political disorders which led to her exile from Lesbus. Alcaeus was said, perhaps wrongly, to be her lover. The story is based on the verses quoted by Aristotle in his *Rhetoric*,[47] "pure Sappho, violet-weaving and gently smiling, I would fain tell you something did not shame prevent me," to which Sappho replied, "If your desire were of things good or fair, and your tongue were not mixing a draught of ill words, then would not shame possess your eye, but you would make your plea outright" (Edmonds). Tradition even in classic times represented her as beloved by Anacreon also,[48] but the bard of Teos flourished at least fifty years after the Lesbian poetess. Archilochus and Hipponax, the famous iambic satiric poets, the former dead before Sappho was born, the latter born after she was dead, were also represented as her lovers by Diphilus,[49] the Athenian comic playwright in his play *Sappho*. But as Athenaeus in the third century A.D. said, "I rather fancy he was joking."

Mackail says that "she was married and had one or more children," and many of the new fragments, as well as Ovid, indicate this. A fragment long known says:

> I *have a maid, a bonny maid,*
> As *dainty as the golden flowers,*
> My *darling Cleïs. Were I paid*

[27]

*All Lydia, and the lovely bowers
Of Cyprus, 'twould not buy my maid.*

(TUCKER)

Professor Prentice [50] translates this fragment
(E. 130), "there is a pretty little girl named
Cleïs whom I love," etc., and says that it does
not refer to her own daughter. But there is
no word for love in the Greek passage, and the
ancient interpretation of Maximus of Tyre [51] is
preferable, especially as Cleïs is definitely mentioned by Suidas and as the name reappears as
that of a young woman in another of the old
fragments and in one of the new pieces.[52] The
matter seems now to be settled by the recent
discovery on a papyrus (about 200 A.D.) of a
new late prose biography of Sappho which is
so important a source for her life that a literal
translation of it is here given, especially as it
is not in Edmonds' *Lyra Graeca*.[53]

"Sappho by birth was a Lesbian and of the
city of Mytilene and her father was Scamandrus
or according to some Scamandronymus. And
she had three brothers, Eurygyius, Larichus,
and the eldest, Charaxus, who sailed to Egypt
and as an associate with a certain Doricha spent
very much on her; but Sappho loved more

[28]

Larichus, who was young. She had a daughter Cleïs with the same name as her own mother. She has been accused by some of being disorderly in character and of being a woman-lover. In shape she seems to have proved contemptible and ugly, for in complexion she was dark, and in stature she was very small; and the same has happened in the case of . . . who was undersized."

The man whom Sappho married, she herself also being a person of some means, was said to be Cercylas, a man of great wealth from the island of Andrus. Cercylas sounds like concocted comic chaff, but we can believe enough of the tradition to say that she was married. A Russian scholar [54] made her a widow at thirty-five.[55] Thereafter she sought for love and companionship among the girls whom she made members of her salon and instructed in the arts.

Sappho must have had a wonderful personality or she could not have attracted so many pupils and companions whom she trained to chant or sing in the choruses for the marriage ceremony and for other occasions. She was president of the world's first woman's club. It was a *thiasos* or a kind of sacred sorority to which the members were bound by special ties and regulations.

We have a long list of the members who were
her friends and pupils, not only from Lesbus
but from Miletus, Colophon, Pamphylia, and
even Salamis and Athens. For some of them
she had an ardent passion. When they left her,
she missed them terribly (E. 43, 44, 46). "Is
it possible for any maid on earth to be far apart
from the woman she loves?" She was so jealous at times that she spited her wrath on her
rivals, especially Gorgo and Andromeda. She
"had enough of Gorgo," and she scolds Atthis
for having come to hate the thought of her and
for flitting after Andromeda in her stead (E. 55,
81). Suidas tells us that she had three companions or friends, Atthis, Telesippa, and Meg-
ara, to whom she was slanderously declared to
be attached by an impure affection; and that
her pupils or disciples were Anagora (Anactoria)
of Miletus, Gongyla (the dumpling) of Colophon, Euneica of Salamis. Ovid mentions
Atthis, Cydro, and Anactoria, the name which
Swinburne took for his poem in which he welded
together many of Sappho's fragments with fine
expression and passionate thought. Maximus
of Tyre (xxiv, 9) says: "What Alcibiades,
Charmides, and Phaedrus were to Socrates,
Gyrinna, Atthis and Anactoria were to Sappho,

and what his rival craftsmen, Prodicus, Gorgias,
Thrasymachus and Protagoras were to Socrates, that Gorgo and Andromeda were to Sappho,
who sometimes takes them to task and at others
refutes them and dissembles with them exactly
like Socrates" (Edmonds). Philostratus in his
Life of Apollonius of Tyana [56] tells of Sappho's
brilliant pupil Damophyla of Pamphylia who is
said to have had girl-companions like Sappho
and to have composed love-poems and hymns
just as she did, with adaptations from the lectures of her professor. Her own fragments
mention Anactoria, Atthis, Gongyla, Gyrinno
(which perhaps means Little Tadpole),
"Mnasidica, of fairer form than the dainty
Gyrinno" (E. 115), and possibly Eranna.[57]
One fragment says, "Well did I teach Hero of
Gyara, the fleetly-running maid" (E. 73). If
this is the famous Hero of the Hero and Leander
story so often pictured in Greek art and on coins
of Abydus, Sappho knew the story of two king's
children who loved one another long before the
days of the painter Apelles.[58] Sappho's school
of poetry in modern times has been prettily
pictured in a painting by Hector Leroux (p. 118),
but the best representation of what her school
may have been is given by Alma Tadema (Pl. 1)

in his academic and learned classical painting
"Sappho" in the Walters' Art Gallery in Baltimore. Archaic Greek inscriptions, of interest
to the specialist in epigraphy, can be read on
the marble seats of the theatre at Mytilene
represented in the picture, — the names of Erinna
of Telos, Gyrinno, Anactoria of Miletus, Atthis,
Gongyla of Colophon, Dika (short for Mnasidica), and others. I quote the beautiful appreciation which Professor Gildersleeve has
published:[59]

"A semi-circle of marble seats, veined and
stained, a screen of olive trees that fling their
branches against the sky, and against the sapphire
seas, a singing man, a listening woman, whose
listening is so intense that nothing else in the
picture seems to listen — not the wreathed girl in
flowered robe who stands by her and rests her hand
familiarly on her shoulder. Not she, for though
she holds a scroll in her other hand, the full face,
the round eyes, show a soul that matches wreathed
head and flowered robe. She is the pride of life.
Nor she on the upper seat, who props her chin with
her hand and partly hides her mouth with her fingers
and lets her vision reach into the distance of her
own musings. Nor her neighbor whose composed
attitude is that of a regular church-goer who has
learned the art of sitting still and thinking of
nothing. Nor yet the remotest figure — she who
has thrown her arms carelessly on the back of the
seat and is looking out on the waters as if they

[32]

would bring her something. A critic tells us that the object of the poet is to enlist Sappho's support in a political scheme of which he is the leader, if not the chief prophet, and he has come to Sappho's school in Lesbos with the hope of securing another voice and other songs to advocate the views of his party. The critic seems to have been in the artist's secret, and yet Alma Tadema painted better than he knew. Alkaios is not trying to win Sappho's help in campaign lyrics. The young poet is singing to the priestess of the Muses a new song with a new rhythm, and as she hears it, she feels that there is a strain of balanced strength in it she has not reached: it is the first revelation to her of the rhythm that masters her own. True, when Alkaios afterwards sought not her help in politics, but her heart in love, and wooed her in that rhythm, she too had caught the music and answered him in his own music."

III. THE LEGENDARY FRINGE

SAPPHO'S PHYSICAL APPEARANCE, THE PHAON STORY, THE VICE IDEA

SO FAR we have been dealing with ascertained facts, reasonable inferences as to other facts, and strong probabilities: in a word, with the real Sappho so far as her history can be made out with at least some measure of certainty. There is, however, a legendary fringe attaching to every great outstanding personality. It is one of the penalties of personal or literary greatness to become the centre of fanciful stories, personal detraction, misrepresentation, and wild legends often conceived in a most grotesque and improbable fashion. To all this Sappho is no exception. First the question will be discussed whether she was a dwarf. The famous and far-flung story of Phaon and the Leucadian Leap will then claim our mention, and thirdly a word must be said about her character.

According to Damocharis [60] Sappho had a beautiful face and bright eyes. The famous

line of Alcaeus refers to her gentle smile. So
Burns in his *Pastoral Poetry* says, "In thy sweet
voice, Barbauld, survives even Sappho's flame."
Plato calls her beautiful as does many another
writer, though the epithet may refer, as Maximus
of Tyre says, to the beauty of her lyrics, one of
which practically says long before Goldsmith,
"handsome is that handsome does" (E. 58).
The word which Alcaeus employs does not nec-
essarily mean that she had violet tresses as
Edmonds translates it. It has generally been
rendered as violet-weaving, and it is to be regretted that P. N. Ure without evidence, in his
excellent book entitled *The Greek Renaissance*
(London, 1921), tells us that Sappho had black
hair, even if Mrs. Browning does speak of
"Sappho, with that gloriole of ebon hair on
calmèd brows." Tall blondes were popular in
ancient days and Sappho was neither divinely
tall nor most divinely fair. But the ancient
busts, the representations of her as full-sized,
on coins of Lesbos and on many Greek vases,
belie the idea of the rhetorical Maximus of
Tyre who in the second century A.D. labelled
her "small and dark," an idea that occurs also
in the new papyrus which we have already
quoted. Some have even interpreted her name

as derived from Ψᾶφος, "Little Pebble," i.e., short of stature. Undoubtedly the epithet of Maximus reflects the Roman perverted idea which finds expression in Ovid's apology for her appearance. The scholiast on Lucian's *Portraits* [61] is repeating the same source when he says " physically, Sappho was very ill-favored, being small and dark, like a nightingale with ill-shapen wings enfolding a tiny body." The famous fragment,

> *This little creature, four feet high,*
> *Cannot hope to touch the sky,*
>
> (EDMONDS)

may not refer to Sappho, and if it does, we must remember, that Edmonds' new reading is doubtful. Perhaps Horace was thinking of this line when he wrote [62]

> *sublimi feriam sidera vertice,*

which recalls Tennyson's

> *Old Horace! I will strike, said he,*
> *The stars with head sublime.*
>
> (EPILOGUE)

Edmonds forces the meaning of the Greek to get even four feet out of his new restoration.

Sappho was surely taller than that and there is
no evidence earlier than Roman days to justify
even Swinburne's

> *The small dark body's Lesbian loveliness*
> *That held the fire eternal.*

In any case Sappho was no dwarf, otherwise
her deformity would not have escaped the
notice of the Athenian comic mud-slingers and
scandal-mongers who did so much to spoil her
good name. Such is the traditional, not the
real, human, historical Sappho of the sixth
century B.C.

The story of Sappho's love for Phaon is
patently mythological, as indicated by the
legend of his transformation by Aphrodite from
an old man into a handsome youth. There can
be only slight historic foundation for connecting Sappho with him and making Sicily the
scene of their first meeting. An inscription on
the Parian marble in Oxford says: "When Cri-
tius the First was archon at Athens Sappho
fled from Mytilene and sailed to Sicily." The
date is uncertain as there is a lacuna in the
inscription, but it is between 604 and 594 B.C.,
perhaps about 598. The recently discovered
hymn to Hera, *Longing for Lesbus*, lends support

to this story of exile. She may have been banished by Pittacus for engaging like Alcaeus in political intrigues. She probably returned to Lesbus under the amnesty of 581, as her grave is often mentioned as in Lesbus. There is even a tradition preserved by the English traveller Pococke that her own sepulchral urn was once in the Turkish mosque of the castle of Mytilene. We have already cited one or two fragments which seem to show that she had more than reached middle age. She was old enough to feel that she should not re-marry, especially if she had to choose one younger than herself.[63] Fragment (E. 99) is in the style of Shakespeare's "Crabbed age and youth cannot live together." Nowhere in her poems is there any evidence that she committed suicide for love of Phaon, but as her name has started this legend we must speak of it in some detail. The famous fragment (E. 108), to judge from the context where it is quoted in connection with Socrates' death, seems to give her last words: "It is not right that there be mourning in the house of poetry; this befits us not."

Now let us discuss the supposititious love affair, to which we have referred, about which I share the ancient and modern Lesbian doubt.

The ancients tell of Sappho's unrequited love for the ferryman prototype of St. Christopher, the beautiful Phaon. The story is well given in Servius' *précis* of Turpilius' Latin paraphrase of Menander, [64] though he does not mention Sappho by name: "Phaon, who was a ferryman plying for hire between Lesbus (others say he was from Chios [65]) and the mainland, one day ferried over for nothing the Goddess Venus in the guise of an old woman, and received from her for the service an alabaster box of unguent, the daily use of which made women fall in love with him. Among those who did so was one who in her disappointment is said to have thrown herself from Mount Leucates, and from this came the custom now in vogue of hiring people once a year to throw themselves from that place into the sea." (Edmonds). But neither Phaon nor anything connected with Phaon is mentioned in any of Sappho's fragments, though Francis Fawkes and others have connected Phaon's name with the Hymn to Aphrodite. A writer of the second century B.C., Palaephatus,[66] makes the very inconsistent statement that "this is the Phaon in whose honor as a lover many a song has been written by Sappho." Nor is there any allusion to

Sappho's curing her passion by leaping from the white Leucadian cliff. Athenaeus [67] and Suidas go so far as to say that the victim was another Sappho, and even in the late lists of Leucadian leapers, in Photius, Sappho is not included. Who first conjured up a Phaon, we know not, but the story belongs to folk-lore, and Phaon appears on Greek vases of the time and style of Meidias, who is dated by most archaeologists toward the end of the fifth century B.C., much earlier than Plato's play (392 B.C.). His indifference to the many ladies who are making love to him is well portrayed, especially on vases (Pl. 4, 5) in Florence and Palermo (p. 107) [68]. The fair Phaon, Aphrodite's shining star ($\phi\acute{a}\omega\nu$ = shining), is only another *avatar* of Adonis, who appears in similar style on similar vases, one even found in the same grave with a Phaon vase. Phaon, I believe, is as old as the fifth century; but the story of Sappho's leap transferred to the white cliffs in the south of the white island of Leucas, the modern Cape Ducato, is later. The Cape is also called Santa Maura, some two hundred feet high, and even to-day this rock of desperation is haunted by Sappho's ghost and known as Sappho's Leap (Pl. 6). The legend of the Les-

[40]

bian's leap first occurs in the poet of the Old Comedy, Plato, who wrote the play called *Phaon*. Later in the New Comedy, Menander was probably adorning an old tale to point a contemporary moral when he produced his *Leucadia* of which Turpilius, a contemporary of Terence, wrote a Latin paraphrase. A few anapaestic lines are preserved by Strabo, who speaks of the Leucadian Cliff:

Where Sappho 'tis said the first of the world
In her furious chase of Phaon so haughty
All maddened with longing plunged down from the height
*   Of the shimmering rock.*

(D. M. R.)

Antiphanes probably told the story in both his *Leucadius* and his *Phaon;* and Cratinus must have mentioned Phaon, for Athenaeus [69] tells us that he told how Aphrodite, beloved by Phaon, concealed him among the fair wild lettuce, just as other writers say Adonis was hidden.

The practice of abandoned lovers taking the leap may possibly have been known even in Sappho's day, for Stesichorus tells of a girl throwing herself from a cliff near Leucas because a youth had scorned her. By the time of Anacreon (550 B.C.), the leap had become the symbol of a love passion that could no longer be borne; "Lifted up from the Leucadian rock, I dive into the hoary wave, drunk with Love." It is the same old story told at every summer resort about some place called Lover's Leap, but in Anacreon nothing is said about drowning. And legend [70] says that sometimes wings or feathers were attached to the person jumping off the cliff to lighten the fall. In any case the leap, legendary or not, was not suicide but a desperate remedy, killing or curing, for hopeless love. We hear of many who survived the expiatory leap.

In a stucco fresco [71] (Pl. 7) (not later than 40 A.D.) in the half dome of the apse at one end of the underground building in Rome near the Porta Maggiore, which served for the cult of some secret neo-Pythagorean sect or possibly as a temple of the Muses or possibly only as the underground summer abode of an enthusiast over Greek poets like the newly discovered underground rooms of the Homeric enthusiast at Pompeii, we have possibly an illustration of the Leucadian leap, at least in symbolism, as personifying the parting of the image of the soul. Sappho, lyre in hand, is springing from the misty cliff, which Ausonius mentions in his sixth idyl (cf.

p. 131), and below in the sea is a Triton spreading out a garment to break her fall. Opposite on a height stands Apollo, who had a temple on the spot and to whom according to Ovid's *Fifteenth Heroic Epistle* Sappho promised to dedicate her lyre if he was propitious. Ovid is the first writer from whom we have the story in detail. It was often used in later literature, as we shall see in a succeeding chapter. Many know Pope's translation of Ovid,[72] but if my readers desire to read an imaginative and humorous circumstantial account of Sappho's leap, on which the modern popular idea is mostly based, they may find it in Addison's *Spectator*, No. 233, November 27, 1711.

The moral purity of Sappho shines in its own light. She expresses herself, no doubt, in very passionate language, but passionate purity is a finer article than the purity of prudery, and Sappho's passionate expressions are always under the control of her art. A woman of bad character and certainly a woman of such a variety of bad character as scandal (cf. p. 128 and note 147) has attributed to Sappho might express herself passionately and might run on indefinitely with erotic imagery. But Sappho is never erotic. There is no language to be

[43]

found in her songs which a pure woman might not use, and it would be practically impossible for a bad woman to subject her expressions to the marvellous niceties of rhythm, accent, and meaning which Sappho everywhere exhibits. Immorality and loss of self-control never subject themselves to perfect literary and artistic taste. It is against the nature of things that a woman who has given herself up to unnatural and inordinate practices which defy the moral instinct and throw the soul into disorder, practices which harden and petrify the soul, should be able to write in perfect obedience to the laws of vocal harmony, imaginative portrayal, and arrangement of the details of thought. The nature of things does not admit of such an inconsistency. Sappho's love for flowers, moreover, affords another luminous testimony. A bad woman as well as a pure woman might love roses, but a bad woman does not love the small and hidden wild flowers of the field, the dainty anthrysc and the clover, as Sappho did. There is, moreover, in a life of vice something narrowing as well as coarsening. An imagination which like Sappho's sees in a single vision the moonlight sweeping the sea, breaking across the shore and illuminating wide stretches of landscape with life-giving light, and in the midst of all this far-spreading glory sees and personifies the spirit of the night, listening to the moanings of homesickness and repeating them with far-flung voice to those across the sea, — an imagination with such a marvellous range as this is never given to the child of sodden vice. Here once more is a woman who made it her life business to adorn and even to glorify lawful wedlock, and carried on this occupation in a sympathetic and delightful strain of dance and song which, however passionate in their expression, contain no impure words. It is simply unthinkable that such a woman should be perpetually destroying the very foundations of her own ideals.

IV. THE WRITINGS OF SAPPHO

THE NUMBER of poems or fragments (Pl. 8) of Sappho has increased from a hundred and twenty in Volger's edition (1810) to a hundred and ninety-one in Edmonds. "Though few they are roses," and a marvellous vitality and mentality permeates their mangled and marred members. Sappho probably had her own collection of her poems, but they were surely not published in a large edition as has sometimes been said. An introductory poem is possibly preserved on an Attic vase, but even of that we cannot be sure. In Roman days there were two editions, one arranged according to subject and the other according to metre, both based on some Alexandrian source much earlier than the book *On the Metres of Sappho*, published by Dracon of Stratonicea about 180 A.D. Sappho wrote many forms of literature in many different metres, cult hymns or odes, marriage songs, scolia or drinking songs, songs of love and friendship, besides her nine books of lyrics, epigrams, elegies, none of which has survived or been described by any other

[46]

author, iambics, monodies, and funeral songs like that for Adonis. The Athenian dramatists even pictured her as proposing puzzles and riddles. Colombarius, as quoted by Meursius in his notes on Hesychius, called Sappho the poetess of the Trojans, the meaning of which has recently been made clear by the discovery of the *Marriage of Hector and Andromache*.

The first poem is the *Ode to Aphrodite* which was cited by Dionysius of Halicarnassus for its finished and brilliant style, — the style used by Euripides among the tragedians and by Isocrates among the orators. Though the rhythm, ardor, terseness, and noble simplicity can be given in no translation,[73] nearly every lover of Greek lyrics has tried his hand at it. Ambrose Philips made thirty-four words out of the first stanza which in the Greek has only sixteen; Merivale found forty-three words necessary; but Tucker and Leonard with strict compression and simplicity manage to translate with twenty-three; Gildersleeve in an unpublished version which I also quote here, and Fairclough use twenty-four:

BROIDERED-THRONED *goddess, O Aphrodite,*
Child of Zeus, craft-weaving, I do beseech thee,
Do not crush my soul with distress and sorrow,
Wholly my mistress.

[47]

Rather come, if ever didst come aforetime,
Hearkening to my cry from afar in mercy;
And didst leave the palace of thine own father
        Golden and gorgeous;

And didst yoke thy chariot, swift thy sparrows
Drew thee, beauteous sparrows, to earth's dark
        surface,
Moving quick their wings from the height of heaven
        Through the mid ether.

Soon their journey's end was attained and smiling
Blessed goddess, smiling with heavenly visage,
Thou didst ask of me what it was I suffer'd,
        Why I invoked thee,

What it was I wished to receive of all things,
Maddened in my soul, 'Who is he thou seekest,
Whom shall I ensnare for my darling Sappho?
        Who is it grieves thee?'

'Nay, if thou but flee he will soon pursue thee,
If he get no presents, he'll give thee presents,
If thou love him not, he will love thee quickly,
        E'en if thou wilt not.'

Come then now again and relieve me, goddess,
From my carking cares and whate'er my spirit
Longeth for accomplish, and on my side do
        Battle, my mistress;

(GILDERSLEEVE)

or, with the translation of doves for sparrows:

[48]

GUILE-WEAVING *child of Zeus, who art*
Immortal, throned in radiance, spare,
O Queen of Love, to break my heart
        With grief and care.
But hither come, as thou of old,
When my voice reached thine ear afar,
Didst leave thy father's hall of gold,
        And yoke thy car,
And through mid air their whirring wing
Thy bonny doves did swiftly ply
O'er the dark earth, and thee did bring
        Down from the sky.
Right soon they came, and thou, blest Queen,
A smile upon thy face divine,
Didst ask what ail'd me, what might mean
        That call of mine.
'What would'st thou have, with heart on fire,
Sappho?' thou saidst. 'Whom pray'st thou me
To win for thee to fond desire?
        Who wrongeth thee?
Soon shall he seek, who now doth shun;
Who scorns thy gifts, shall gifts bestow;
Who loves thee not, shall love anon,
        Wilt thou or no.'
So come thou now, and set me free
From carking cares; bring to full end
My heart's desire; thyself O be
        My stay and friend!

                                    (TUCKER) [74]

[49]

Here follow two translations where "he" is changed to "she" in the sixth stanza. The controversy as to the sex of the belovèd turns on the admission or omission of a single letter in the Greek.

DEATHLESS *Aphrodite, throned in flowers,*
Daughter of Zeus, O terrible enchantress,
With this sorrow, with this anguish, break my spirit,
Lady, not longer!

Hear anew the voice!   O hear and listen!
Come, as in that island dawn thou camest,
Billowing in thy yokèd car to Sappho
Forth from thy father's

Golden house in pity! . . . . I remember:
Fleet and fair thy sparrows drew thee, beating
Fast their wings above the dusky harvests,
Down the pale heavens,

Lighting anon!   And thou, O blest and brightest,
Smiling with immortal eyelids, asked me:
'Maiden, what betideth thee?   Or wherefore
Callest upon me?

What is hers the longing more than others,
Here in this mad heart?   And who the lovely
One belovèd thou wouldst lure to loving?
Sappho, who wrongs thee?'

[50]

'See, if now she flies, she soon must follow;
Yes, if spurning gifts, she soon must offer;
Yes, if loving not, she soon must love thee,
    Howso unwilling. . . .'

Come again to me! O now! Release me!
End the great pang! And all my heart desireth
Now of fulfilment, fulfil! O Aphrodite,
    Fight by my shoulder!

                (W. E. LEONARD, unpublished)

RICHLY throned, O deathless one, Aphrodite,
Child of Zeus, enchantress-queen, I beseech thee
Let not grief nor harrowing anguish master,
    Lady, my spirit.

Ah! come hither. Erstwhile indeed thou heardest
When afar my sorrowful cry of mourning
Smote thine ears, and then from thy father's
    mansions
      Golden thou camest,

Driving forth thy chariot, and fair birds bore thee
Speeding onward over the earth's dark shadows,
Waving oft their shimmering plumes thro' heaven's
    Ether encircling.

Quickly drew they nigh me, and thou, blest presence,
Sweetest smile divine on thy face immortal,
Thou didst seek what sorrow was mine to suffer,
    Wherefore I called thee.

What my soul, too, craved with intensest yearning,
Frenzy's fire enkindling. 'Now whom,' thou criest,
'Wouldst thou fain see led to thy love, or who, my
Sappho, would wrong thee?'

'Though she flees thee now, yet she soon shall woo
thee,
Though thy gifts she scorneth, she soon shall bring
gifts;
Though she loves thee not, yet she soon shall love thee,
Yea, though unwilling.'

Come, ah! come again, and from bitter anguish
Free thy servant. All that my heart is craving,
That fulfil, O goddess. Thyself, my champion,
Aid in this conflict.

(H. RUSHTON FAIRCLOUGH)

The second ode, quoted in a mutilated con-
dition by the treatise *On the Sublime*, is even
more difficult to translate. As Wordsworth
says, here

the Lesbian Maid
With finest touch of passion swayed
Her own Aeolian lute.

In its rich Aeolian dialect the ode glows with
true Greek fire. Sappho's words are clear but
far from cold. They are a sea of glass, but a

[52]

sea of glass mingled with fire such as the Patmos seer saw from his island not far from Sappho's Lesbian home. They enable us to understand why Byron in *Don Juan* speaks of "the isles of Greece where burning Sappho loved and sung." This is what Swinburne means, when he speaks of the fire eternal and in his *Sapphics* says that about her " shone a light of fire as a crown for ever." We know from Plutarch [75] that an ancient physician, Erasistratus, included this ode (which has influenced realistic descriptions of passion from Euripides and Theocritus to Swinburne and Sara Teasdale) in his book of diagnoses as a compendium of all the symptoms of corroding emotions. He applied this psychological test whenever Antiochus looked on Stratonice. "There appeared in the case of Antiochus all those symptoms which Sappho mentions: the choking of the voice, the feverish blush, the obscuring of vision, profuse sweat, disordered and tumultuous pulse and finally, when he was completely overcome, bewilderment, amazement and pallor." Perhaps Sappho was influenced by Homer's [76] description of fear and she herself surely suggested such symptoms to Lucretius. [77] We must regard the ode primarily as a literary product, but its pathological picture of passion is hardly secondary. Even if the symptoms seem appalling to our cold and unexpressive northern blood, we must remember that this physical perturbation, as Tucker calls it, was in no way strange to the ancients. Gildersleeve put it well in his unpublished lecture on Sappho, which he so kindly placed at my disposal and to which I am greatly indebted: "if a Greek melted, he melted with a fervent heat, and if this is true of the average Greek how much more was it true of an Aeolian and an Aeolian woman, and of Sappho most Aeolian of all." Byron refers to this ode when he says in *Don Juan:*

> *Catullus scarcely has a decent poem,*
> I *don't think Sappho's Ode a good example,*
> *Although Longinus tells us there is no hymn*
> *Where the sublime soars forth on wings more ample.*

With regard to Catullus' rendering (LI), Swinburne in his *Notes on Poems and Reviews*, speaking of his poem *Anactoria*, says: "Catullus translated or as his countrymen would now say 'traduced' the Ode to Anactoria; a more beautiful translation there never was and will never be; but compared with the Greek, it is colourless and bloodless, puffed out by additions and

[54]

enfeebled by alterations. Let anyone set against
each other the two first stanzas, Latin and Greek,
and pronounce . . . Where Catullus failed I could
not hope to succeed; I tried instead to reproduce in a diluted and dilated form the spirit
of a poem which could not be reproduced in
the body."

Tennyson has given the best paraphrase in
Eleänore:

> I WATCH *thy grace; and in its place*
> My *heart a charmed slumber keeps,*
> While *I muse upon thy face;*
> And *a languid fire creeps*
> Thro' *my veins to all my frame,*
> Dissolvingly *and slowly: soon*
> From *thy rose-red lips my name*
> Floweth; *and then, as in a swoon,*
> With *dinning sound my ears are rife,*
> My *tremulous tongue faltereth,*
> I *lose my color, I lose my breath,*
> I *drink the cup of a costly death,*
> Brimm'd *with delirious draughts of warmest life.*
> I *die with my delight, before*
> I *hear what I would hear from thee.*

The following version I have based mainly on
Edmonds' recent text,[78] with a conjectural restoration of the last stanza, of which only a few
words are preserved in the Greek:

O LIFE *divine! to sit before*
Thee while thy liquid laughter flows
Melodious, and to listen close
To rippling notes from Love's full score.

O *music of thy lovely speech!*
My rapid heart beats fast and high,
My tongue-tied soul can only sigh,
And strive for words it cannot reach.

O *sudden subtly-running fire!*
My ears with dinning ringing sing,
My sight is lost, a blinded thing,
Eyes, hearing, speech, in love expire,

My face pale-green, like wilted grass
Wet by the dew and evening breeze,
Yea, my whole body tremblings seize,
Sweat bathes me, Death nearby doth pass,

Such thrilling swoon, ecstatic death
Is for the gods, but not for me,
My beggar words are naught to thee,
Far-off thy laugh and perfumed breath.

(D.M.R.)

As J. A. K. Thomson says in his recent fas-
cinating book *Greeks and Barbarians* (London
and New York, 1921), "Sappho, in the most
famous of her odes, says that love makes her
'sweat' with agony and look 'greener than

grass.' Perhaps she did not turn quite so green as that, although (commentators nobly observe) she would be of an olive complexion and had never seen British grass. But, even if it contain a trace of artistic exaggeration, the ode as a whole is perhaps the most convincing love-poem ever written.) It breathes veracity. It has an intoxicating beauty of sound and suggestion, and it is as exact as a physiological treatise. The Greeks can do that kind of thing. Somehow we either overdo the 'beauty' or we overdo the physiology. The weakness of the Barbarian, said they, is that he never hits the mean. But the Greek poet seems to do it every time. We may beat them at other things, but not at that. And they do it with so little effort; sometimes, it might happen, with none at all."

The passion of love is the supreme subject of Sappho's songs, as shown by these first two and many a short fragment, as for example (E. 81) where Love is called for the first time in literature "sweet-bitter." Some scholars have credited it to the much later Posidippus, but he and Meleager took the word from Sappho, though it may not have been original even with her. Sappho's order of the compound word is generally reversed in translation, but Sir Edwin

Arnold says "sweetly bitter, sadly dear," and Swinburne in *Tristram of Lyonesse* speaks of "Sweet Love, that are so bitter." Tennyson also has the same order in *Lancelot and Elaine* (pp. 205–206). To Sappho love is a second death, and in the second ode death itself seems not very far away. The Greek words for swooning are mostly metaphors from death, and so we are not surprised when we read that like death love relaxes every limb and sweeps one away in its giddy swirling, a sweet-bitter resistless wild beast. Here is Sir Sidney Colvin's translation (*John Keats*, 1917, p. 332): "Love the limb-loosener, the bitter-sweet torment, the wild beast there is no withstanding, never harried a more helpless victim." Another fragment (E. 54) also shows the power of love:

> *Love tossed my heart as the wind*
> *That descends on the mountain oaks.*
>
> (EDMONDS)

Sappho's range of subjects is much greater than the personal emotions of love, though very personal and individual feelings predominate. She touches almost every field of human experience, so that there is much in her scant fragments to bring her near to us. The wail against

[58]

ingratitude comes home to those high-strung
natures who do good to others but are sensitive
to every wrong when they have the unfortunate
experience of learning that one's friends are
sometimes one's own worst enemies. "Those
harm me most by whom I have done well"
(Mackail). But she is not one of those who
bear a grudge long, her heart is for peace. One
of the few ethical fragments, as Mackail says,
"is a speech of delicate self-abasement, spoken
with the effect of a catch in the voice and
tears behind the eyes;" "No rancour in this
breast runs wild, I have the heart of a child."
Sappho's love of sermonizing is seen in her
commandment: "when anger swells in the
heart, restrain the idly barking tongue." From
Aristotle's *Rhetoric* Edmonds (91) reconstructs
another fragment:

> *Death is an ill; the Gods at least think so,*
> *Or else themselves had perished long ago.*

In another fragment of a different nature (E.
120) we read: "Stand up, look me in the face
as friend to friend and unveil the charm that
is in thy eyes." In other fragments we enter
a Lesbian lady's home and see woman's love
of dress, — no short skirt for her, for they

"wrapped her all around with soft cambric"
(E. 105). "A motley gown of fair Lydian work
reached down to her feet" (E. 20), or, if we
believe Pollux (VII. 93), it is the Greek love of
fine shoes. No Lesbian butchery for her tender
feet, but she must wear soft luxurious Lydian
slippers: "A broidered strap of fair Lydian
work covered her feet." Punning on the name
of Timas (precious), another fragment, which
perhaps refers to a statue of Aphrodite in
Sappho's home, seems to dote on fancy hand-
kerchiefs; "and hanging on either side thy face
the purple handkerchief which Timas sent for
thee from Phocaea, a precious gift from a precious giver" (E. 87).[79] The fragment (E. 21),
"shot with a thousand hues," refers to dress
rather than to the rainbow. The sight of
beautiful gowns thrilled her: "Come you back,
my rosebud Gongyla, in your milk-white gown."
Again she says: "Many are the golden brace-
lets and the purple robes, aye and the fine
smooth broideries, indeed a richly varied bride-
gift; and without number also are the silver
goblets and the ornaments of ivory" (E. 66).
She coined new words for women; she calls the
chest in which women keep their perfumes and
like things a *gruté* or hutch (E. 180). Again

she uses (E. 179) the word *Beudos* for a short diaphanous frock or blouse. She is the first to use the word *Chlamys*, where she speaks of Love as "coming from Heaven and throwing off his purple mantle" (E. 69). Blondes were much admired among the fair-haired Lesbians, though Sappho herself was a brunette, and so she herself mentions (E. 189) a kind of box-wood or scytharium-wood with which women dye their hair a golden color. She is fond of cassia and frankincense (E. 66), and she dotes on myrrh and royal perfumes (E. 83). She rebukes the foolish girl who prides herself on her ring.[80] With "a keen swift flicker of woman's jealousy," and well acquainted with the philosophy of clothes and with the new Ionic dresses introduced into Lesbus during her own lifetime at the beginning of the sixth century B.C. from Asia Minor, she jests about her rival Andromeda, the country girl who knows not how to manage the train of her new gown [81] (E. 98):

> *What rustic hoyden ever charmed the soul,*
> *That round her ankles could not kilt her coats!*
>
> (THOMAS DAVIDSON in *Warner's Library of the World's Best Literature*)

[61]

There is an intimate love of the loveliness of nature in Sappho, as we should expect of one resident on an island under Ionian skies where, as Herodotus (I. 142) says, "the climate and seasons are the most beautiful of any cities in the world." "The many garlanded earth puts on her broidery" (E. 133). "Thus of old did the dainty feet of Cretan maidens dance pat to the music beside some lovely altar, pressing the soft smooth bloom of the grass (E. 114). As Thomas Davidson has so well said: "every hour of the day comes to Sappho with a fresh surprise." We lie down for a noonday siesta in " a murmurous, blossomy June," as Stebbing puts it, in the orchard of the nymphs where (E. 4),

around
Through boughs of the apple
Cool waters sound.
From the rustling leaves
Drips sleep to the ground.

(Unpublished, RHYS CARPENTER) [82]

In the Greek, as Edwin Cox says, "the sound of the words, the repetition of long vowels particularly omega, the poetic imagery of the whole and the drowsy cadence of the last two words give this fragment a combination of qualities

[62]

probably not surpassed in any language." The
beautiful verses about the pippin on the topmost
branch we shall quote below. In another fragment (E. 3) Sappho sees the stars in a way
which Tennyson echoes when he writes: "As
when in heaven the stars about the moon Look
beautiful." Or again Sappho's love of nature
appears in the line (E. 112): "the moon rose
full and the maidens took their stand about the
altar." In the new *Ode to Atthis* the moon is not
silver (as in E. 3) but rosy-fingered: "after sunset the rosy-fingered moon beside the stars
that are about her, when she spreads her light
o'er briny sea and eke o'er flowery field, while
the dew lies so fair on the ground and the roses
revive and the dainty anthrysc and the melilot
with all its blooms" (E. 86). Recently (1922)
A. C. Benson in *The Reed of Pan* has combined
fragment (E. 3) with the beautiful half stanza
quoted above, under the title *Moonrise:*

The moon high-hung in the hollow night
Resistless pours her silver tide;
Swift, swift the stars withdraw their light,
And their diminished glories hide.

And where cool streams through reed-beds slip,
The breeze through the orchard alley stirs,

[63]

And slumber well-nigh seems to drip
From the dark arms of dusky firs.

In another fragment, which we quote below, Sappho pictures a spring midnight with almost astronomical exactness. She loves the sun: "I have loved daintiness [from childhood] and for me love possesses the brightness and beauty of the sun." William Stebbing in his *Minstrel of Love* expands the two verses into ten, the last "Dazzling my brain with gazing on the Sun." Sappho knows the golden-sandalled and queenly dawn (E. 19, 177). She wrote an ode to Hesperus, the Evening Star, of which we have only the tantalizing beginning, "fairest of all the stars that shine" (E. 32). Another graceful fragment quoted in antiquity to show the charm of repetition (E. 149) [83] on the Evening Star, which comes in Catullus too, has influenced not only Byron in *Don Juan* but Andrew Lang in *Helen of Troy* (II. 4) and especially Tennyson (see p. 206). "That Greek blockhead," as Sir Walter Scott was called, though he knew more Greek than most undergraduate students of Greek to-day, even if he didn't know the Sappho fragment, expresses the same idea in the *Doom of Dever Girl*, "All meet whom day and care divide."

Sappho is fond of birds, the dove, the lovely
or heavenly swallow (E. 122), the nightingale.
The doves drive Aphrodite's car in the first ode
and in E. 16 "their heart grows light and they
slacken the labor of their pinions." Ben Jonson
took from Sappho (E. 138) his line in *The Sad
Shepherd*, "the dear good angel of the spring,
The nightingale," and Swinburne, "The tawny
sweet-winged thing Whose cry was but of
spring." A fragment published even since
Edmonds' book speaks of the "clear-voiced
nightingales." She knows exactly what crickets
do at noon of a summer's day. Listen to their
song (E. 94), rescued from Alcaeus, to whom
Bergk had wrongly ascribed it:

*And clear song from beneath her wings doth raise
When she shouts-down the perpendicular blaze
Of the outspread sunshine of noon.*

(EDMONDS) [84]

We see the woman also in her love of flowers
as well as of birds. Flowers are her favorites and
she worships them with almost the modern
reverence of the Japanese, whom I have sometimes seen saying their morning prayers to a
beautiful bouquet. Take, for example, this
simple but pretty flower-picture of Sappho's
(E. 107):

[65]

I saw one day a-gathering flowers
The daintiest little maid.

(EDMONDS)

She sympathizes with the hyacinth (E. 151), which the shepherd tramples under foot on the mountain, and uses it in one of the most attractive flower-similes in all literature. Listen to this aubade which has been recently found and very tentatively restored (E. 82). It gives a delightful glimpse also of Sappho's ménage:

'Sappho, I swear if you come not forth I will love you no more. O rise and shine upon us and set free your beloved strength from the bed, and then like a pure lily beside the spring hold aloof your Chian robe and wash you in the water. And Cleïs shall bring down from your presses saffron smock and purple robe; and let a mantle be put over you and be crowned with a wreath of flowers tied about your head; and so come, sweet with all the beauty with which you make me mad. And do you, Praxinoa, roast us nuts, so that I may make the maidens a sweeter breakfast; for one of the Gods, child, has vouchsafed us a boon. This very day has Sappho the fairest of all women vowed that she will surely return unto Mytilene the dearest of all towns — return with us, the mother with her children.'

Dearest Atthis, can you then forget all this that happened in the old days? . . . (EDMONDS)

Or take this other example of Sappho's love of flowers which Symonds has expanded into a son-

net too long to quote here.   I give Tucker's new
version:

> Take *sprigs of anise fair*
>   *With soft hands twined,*
> *And round thy bonny hair*
>   *A chaplet bind;*
> *The Muse with smiles will bless*
>   *Thy blossoms gay,*
> *While from the garlandless*
>   *She turns away.*

Sappho speaks of the golden pulses (E. 139):

> [*It was summer when I found you*
>   *In the meadow long ago,*]
> *And the golden vetch was growing*
>   *By the shore.*
>
> (BLISS CARMAN)

Sappho knows the little and common flowers,
the dainty anthrysc and melilot, the violets and
the lilies (E. 86, 83, 82), but, like Pindar, she
especially loves the rose. Meleager's garland of
song assigned the rose to Sappho. She says in
one of the new fragments (E. 83): "with many
a garland of violets and sweet roses mingled, you
have decked my flowing locks as I stood by your
side, and with many a woven necklet made of a
hundred blossoms you have adorned my dainty

[67]

throat." Philostratus in his *Letters* (51) says:
"Sappho loves the rose and always crowns
it with a meed of praise, likening beautiful
maidens to it; and she compares it to the bared
fore-arms of the Graces." Fragment E. 68
says: "Hither pure rose-armed Graces, daugh-
ters of Zeus." Sappho's love of the rose has led
earlier collectors of Sappho's fragments to include among her verses the famous song in
praise of the rose quoted by Achilles Tatius in
his love romance on *Clitophon and Leucippe*,
which Elizabeth Barrett Browning has translated:

IF ZEUS *chose us a King of the Flowers in his mirth,*
  He *would call to the Rose and would royally crown it,*
For *the Rose, ho, the Rose, is the grace of the earth,*
  Is *the light of the plants that are growing upon it.*

For *the Rose, ho, the Rose, is the eye of the flowers,*
  Is *the blush of the meadows that feel themselves
    fair —*
Is *the lightning of beauty that strikes through the
    bowers*
  On *pale lovers who sit in the glow unaware.*

Ho, *the Rose breathes of love! Ho, the Rose lifts the
    cup*
  To *the red lips of Cypris invoked for a guest!*

Ho, the Rose, having curled its sweet leaves for the
world,
Takes delight in the motion its petals keep up,
As they laugh to the wind as it laughs from the west!

Sappho, however, does mention the roses of
Pieria in the famous lines spoken with characteristic teacher's tone, almost in the manner of
Mrs. Poyser. According to Plutarch, in one
passage, the verses are addressed to a wealthy
woman, in another passage,[85] to a woman of no
refinement or learning; according to Stobaeus,[86]
to a woman of no education; probably it was
some rich but uncultured Lesbian girl, who
would not go to the Lesbian Smith or Vassar
or Bryn Mawr:

Thou shalt die and be laid low in the grave, hidden
from mortal ken
Unremembered, and no song of the Muse wakens thy
name again;
No Pierian rose brightens thy brow, lost in the name-
less throng,
Thy dark spirit shall flit forth like a dream, bodiless
ghosts among.

(SHOREY)

For another expanded version by Swinburne in
his *Anactoria* I must refer to Wharton. Sappho

[69]

had known and loved the wee wee maiden
Atthis when she was an awkward school girl,
but now in the bloom of beauty after a sad
parting the fickle Atthis has flitted away to another woman's college and clean forgotten
Sappho for a rival teacher, Andromeda; "I
loved you, Atthis, long ago, when my own girlhood was still all flowers, and you — you
seemed to me a small ungainly child" (E. 48).[87]
"So you hate to think of me, Atthis; 'Tis all
Andromeda now" (Edmonds).

Lesbus was a land of flowers, of the rose and
the violet, "a land rich in corn and oil and wine,
in figs and olives, in building-wood and tinted
marble," as Tucker says. But this triangular
island (about thirty-five by twenty-five miles)
had mountains rising from two to three thousand
feet at its corners and two deep fiords on its
southern coast. From the northern coast
Sappho must often have looked across the short
seven miles of laughing sea upon Troyland and
thought of the Homeric poems in which Lesbus
played such an important rôle.[88] The air like
that of Athens as described by Pindar, with a
glamor wreathing such cities as Smyrna, was
so translucent that in the northeast across the
dividing sea many-fountained Ida could easily

be seen. It is perhaps an accident that there is
so little mention of mountain or sea in Sappho.
But she was no "landlubber," as Professor
Allinson would have us believe.[89] Pindar and the
other lyric poets were acquainted with the sea
and so must Sappho have known it, as she daily
saw the ships fly in and out of their haven on
white wings (cf. first stanza of poem on p. 82).
In one of the new fragments (E. 86) we
have a marvellous picture of the sea in
the last stanza of a poem which otherwise,
with its love of flowers, with the beautiful simile
of the rosy-fingered moon, is one of the most
perfect things in literature. The telepathic and
telegraphic sympathy of Sappho startles us and
the wireless message sent by night across the
severing sea, whose sigh you can hear in the
original Greek, anticipates the modern radio.[90]
As this is a memory poem, and *Anactoria*, like
Hallam, is "lost," for the time being at least,
I have followed as a model Tennyson's *In
Memoriam* in metre, stanza, and rhyming. The
first line seems to be "remembered" in rhyme
as it were after the interval during which the
second and third lines have been made and
rhymed.

[71]

SAPPHO'S GIRL FRIEND ACROSS
THE SEA

ATTHIS, *in Sardis far away*
　　Anactoria dear to thee
　　And dear indeed alike to me
Now dwells, but hither often stray

Her thoughts sent usward by the power
　　That lives anew the life she loved
　　When thou her glorious goddess proved, —
Thy songs her joy at every hour.

You were her sun, now set too soon;
　　Among the Lydian dames she shines
　　As, after sunset, glow the lines
Of light the rosy-fingered moon

Throws on her retinue of stars
　　Spreading a far-flung lane of beams
　　That gleams the salt sea o'er and streams
Across the rocky shore that bars

In vain the light that floods its gloom,
　　And leaping landward bathes the fields
　　Where many a flower its beauty yields
With fragrant variegated bloom.

Full fair the dew springs forth and holds
　　The light, the roses lift their heads,
　　The dainty anthryscs quit their beds,
The clover, honey-rich, unfolds.

[72]

Through all this beauty, hard unrest
    And longing crushing like a stone
    Her tender heart, ofttimes alone
She wanders with a weighted breast.

She cannot calm her quivering lip
    And through the balmy, scented dark
    She cries aloud we must embark
And thither come on some swift ship.

Full clear her words to thee and me,
    For night with all her many ears
    Their ardent sound full gladly hears
And sends us o'er the severing sea.

                   (D. M. R.)

This ode alone marks Sappho as a great poetess. The reasons are: (1) the loving notice of little and common flowers, (2) the comparison of Anactoria when surrounded by other women to the moon in the midst of her surrounding stars, the bold personification of the moon secured by the use of the single figure "rosy-fingered," (3) sudden and masterful survey of land and sea, (4) the successful centering of attention upon Anactoria's homesickness even in the midst of such far-reaching beauty of land and sea, (5) the remarkably forceful portrayal of what in our day we call thought-transference as seen, for example, in Tennyson's *Aylmer's Field* or *Enoch Arden*, (6) and not least important, the simplicity and sharpness of outline displayed in the imagery. | "Night" is a vague, widely diffused, mystic thing, but Sappho makes us see her a thing of many ears and one of them close to Anactoria's face. Night does not send a mystic intimation such as Tennyson's vibration of light might indicate. But she speaks right out in a clear voice that carries far enough to reach across the sea to Sappho. A seventh reason is the strange, hot emotion of love and sorrow and longing that throbs like a pulse in every line and makes the whole letter a living creature. Milton said and lovers of poetry have always agreed that poetry must be simple, sensuous, and passionate. By sensuous he of course meant expressed in images involving the use of the bodily senses. Is there anything in poetry, ancient or modern, that more exactly meets Milton's requirements than these few lines of Sappho's letter to her girl friend? Now if this is evident to the reader of an English translation, it is vastly more so to one who knowing the meaning of the words has read them in the Greek and then read them again because they were so sweet, and read them a third time

and many times until the music haunts him
like the face of a lover.   This will rank with
Matthew Arnold's verses *To Marguerite* in no. 5
of his series of little poems on *Switzerland:*

> YES! *in the sea of life enisled,*
> *With echoing straits between us thrown*
>
> .   .   .   .
>
> *Now round us spreads the watery plain —*
> *Oh might our marges meet again!*
>
> *Who order'd that their longing's fire*
> *Should be, as soon as kindled, cool'd?*
> *Who renders vain their deep desire?*
> *A God, a God their severance ruled!*
> *And bade betwixt their shores to be*
> *The unplumb'd, salt, estranging sea.*

Sappho's last verse also reminds us of Horace's
Oceano dissociabili [91] and Tennyson's "bond-
breaking sea."   Fragment E. 41 refers to the
mariner at sea in a storm; and E. 66 pictures
a beautiful scene on the sea, where " Hector
and his comrades bring from sacred Thebe and
everflowing Placia, by ship upon the briny sea,
the dainty Andromache of the glancing eye."
(Edmonds)

Sappho's verses are full of color, of bright and
beautiful things.   She ranks with Pindar in her
special devotion to gold, not for its value but

for its fine amber lustre and its permanency
(E. 110). The Cyprian queen of love sits on a
throne of rich color and splendor, with inlaid
wood or metal (E. 1); she "dispenses the nectar
of love in beakers of gold" in what was perhaps
the introductory poem of Sappho's Wedding-
Songs (E. 6):

Come thou, foam-born Kypris, and pour in dainty
Cups of amber gold thy delicate nectar
Subtly mixed with fire that will swiftly kindle
  Love in our bosoms.

(O'HARA'S Love's Banquet)

Aphrodite wears a golden coronal (E. 9), is
herself golden (E. 157), and her handmaid is
golden-shining (E. 24). The Muses are golden
(E. 11), perhaps also the Nereids (E. 36). They
have a golden house (E. 129):

Hither now, O Muses, leaving the golden
House of God, unseen in the azure spaces.
(O'HARA'S Muses)

The dawn is golden-slippered (E. 19); something
or somebody is more golden than gold (E. 60).
"Gold is pure of rust" (E. 109); "Gold is a
child of Zeus; no moth nor worm devours it;
and it overcomes the strongest of mortal hearts"

[76]

(E. 110).[92] Sappho's daughter Cleïs looks like a golden flower (E. 130); "Golden pulse grew on the shore" (E. 139, cf. O'Hara's poem *Golden Pulse*). One of many fragments of interest to the student of Greek life and antiquities speaks of "gold-knuckle bowls" (E. 191).[93] Sappho was cited by Menaechmus of Sicyon in his *Treatise on Artists* as the first to use a lyre called the *pectis*, and she invented the Mixo-Lydian mode, particularly sensual or emotional, which the Greek tragedians copied from her.

Sappho makes allusions to children which are natural and tender (E. 130). In similes she uses children simply and directly as in *The Ode to Hesperus* (E. 149) and in the verse, which may refer to a sparrow and which Catullus imitated, "I flutter like a child after her mother" (E. 142).

Sappho from her tender years was inured to the sorrows as well as the joys of love. Two of her fragments (E. 111, 135), the first perhaps a complete poem, represent the loneliness of a long night spent in vain waiting for a lover. Cipollini (1890) and others have often set these to music. They are popular ballads which Sappho must have used just as Burns did in writing *Auld Lang Syne*. As Tucker says: "It

[77]

is probable that she is setting one such prehistoric lyrical idea to new words or recasting
one such vagrom ditty." He is thinking, I
imagine, of such a Scottish ballad as:

> *Yestreen I made my bed fu' brade*
> *The night I'll make it narrow:*
> *For a' the livelong winter's night*
> *I'll lie twin'd of my marrow.*

There are a score of versions in Italian, some far
from Sappho, and Ronsard's good French version;
and many an American or English poet has tried
his hand at translating the lines,[94] which in the
Greek toll like a curfew bell. All too little
known is the rendering by Alan Seeger, the poet
who was killed in battle on July 4, 1916, in his
poem, *Do You Remember Once?*

> *Under the western-seas*
> *The pale moon settles and the Pleiades.*
> *The firelight sinks: outside the night-winds moan —*
> *The hour advances, and I sleep alone.*

For the Greek silence of nature Seeger substitutes
the sympathy of nature in the moaning of the
night winds. A more literal translation is:

> *Sunk is the moon*
> *The Pleiades are set;*
> *Tis midnight; soon*

[78]

> The hour is past: and yet
> I lie alone —
>
> (TUCKER)

Sappho's verses are purer, simpler than the frank poem of Hester Bancroft on an *August Night:* [95]

> God, the night will never end
> And I, alone discordant and forlorn,
> Unmated, on this love-night of the year!

The other popular song about a girl in love, in a metre which Horace imitated in the twelfth ode of the third book, is as imaginative a description as anything in Coleridge or Keats with whom the Maryland poet, Father Tabb, so aptly compares Sappho. It reminds one of Gretchen's weaving-song in *Faust*, and of the English folksong, "O mother, put my wheel away; I cannot spin to-night." It is beautifully translated by Thomas Moore, in his *Evenings in Greece:*

> [As o'er her loom the Lesbian maid
> In love-sick languor hung her head,
> Unknowing where her fingers strayed,
> She weeping turned away, and said,]

> 'Oh, my sweet mother, 'tis in vain,
>   I cannot weave, as once I wove,
> So wildered is my heart and brain
>   With thinking of that youth I love.'

Many fragments deal with the Greek myths. Sappho is one of the first to tell the story of Adonis, who has his analogy in Phaon. "Woe for Adonis" (E. 25); "Woe for him of the four months' sojourn, Woe for Adonis" (E. 136 uncertain restoration). Another fragment is presumed to be Sappho's and, probably, to be part of a song sung at the Mytilenaean spring-festival of the marriage of Adonis and Aphrodite, of whose counterpart at Alexandria we have an example in the fifteenth idyl of Theocritus, so well translated by Matthew Arnold:

MAIDENS. *Sweet Adonis lies a-dying, Cytherea;*
what's to do?
CYTHEREA. *Beat your breasts and rend your gar-*
ments, maids, is my behest to you.

(EDMONDS)

O'Hara, Bliss Carman, and many another have expanded this lament for Adonis which we know so well from Bion's *Lament for Adonis* and from Shelley's *Adonais*. I quote the poet laureate of Canada:

What shall we do, Aphrodite?
Lovely Adonis is dying.
Ah but we mourn him!

[80]

*Will he return when the Autumn
Purples the earth, and the sunlight
Sleeps in the vineyard?*

*Will he return when the Winter
Huddles the sheep, and Orion
Goes to his hunting?*

*Ah, for thy beauty, Adonis
With the soft springs and the South wind,
Love and desire!*

(BLISS CARMAN)

Sappho's knowledge of literature and legend is also not little. She is well acquainted with Homer, who very much influenced Sappho's language. She knows Helen (E. 38) and her daughter Hermione (E. 44); "Hermione was never such as you are, and just it is to liken you rather to Helen than to a mortal maid." Or take this complete letter to Anactoria (E. 38), who has eloped with a soldier to Sardis, as beautiful a poem as any of Sappho's, if not spoiled in the last stanza by the wrong restoration of some scholars. The news of its discovery caused Mr. Osborn to leap out of bed and say he would fight for Sappho to the last with a pen dipt in poison. It reminds one of *The Song of Solomon I.* 9, "I have compared thee, O my love, to a company of horses in Pharaoh's chariots," or VI. 10, "Who is she that looketh forth as the morning, fair as the moon, clear as the sun, and terrible as an army with banners?" Osborn, Mark Telfair, Marion Mills Miller, T. E. R., and others [178] have given poetic versions in Sapphics of this new poem. Another rendering seems superfluous, but I could not resist the pleasure of adding it, even though in the main less happy than its predecessors. In some of the lines the love of far-off Sappho's meaning has lured me astray from the nearer English anapaest:

'FAIREST *of sights on the dull black earth,' some say,*
'Is *a host of horse in battle array.'*
'A *phalanx on foot,' another will cry,*
'Or *a navy full sail athwart the sky.'*

'But *nay! 'Tis the lover's beloved,' I ween*
And *easy the proof and plain to be seen;*
For *the sum of all beauty had Helen surveyed,*
Yet *of him, as fairest, her choice she made,*

Who *all the honor of Troy's towers destroyed.*
No *thought of child or parent dear alloyed*
Her *love. Its distant dearness led her far astray;*
For *ever 'tis easy to bend a woman's way,*

If only she hold lightly what is near.
See to it thou, Anactoria dear,
That, parted, we thy memory still shall share
Of her whose silent footfall's music fair

Sounds sweeter, and whose face sheds beams more
    bright
Than the noisy flash of the chariot-fight,
Or tramp of footmen on their glittering way
When Lydia's force deploys in full display.

Too well we know 'tis not for man to gain
His heart's desire, — yet sweeter the pain,
Longing for love we once have shared,
Than forgetting how happily then we fared.

(D. M. R.)

Agamemnon is mentioned in one of the new fragments (tentatively restored E. 85), which is an especially beautiful dialogue between Sappho and her dumpling pupil Gongyla, which might be called *Intimations of Immortality:*

INTIMATION OF COMING DEATH

SAPPHO

My COMING *death I plainly now foresee;*
Long to the end of life it cannot be.

GONGYLA

How dost thou such a sad event divine?
Unto thy dear ones pray reveal the sign.

[83]

SAPPHO

In dream to me Death's angel, Hermes, came
Within my chamber; calling me by name,
'Come,' said he, and he touched me with his wand.
And I, of life and strife no longer fond,
Replied: 'I go with gladness, for I swear
By blessed Cypris that no more I care
To live, since love is passing from me. Fain
Am I to die despite my other gain
In wealth and honor. Only do I plead
To field Elysian, whither thou didst lead
Atrides Agamemnon and the flower
Of the Achaeans, take me in my hour,
And set me in that dewy vale to bloom,
Perchance again with beauty and perfume
That love invite, although with kindlier fate —
Not of ignoble souls, but of the great.'

(Adaptation by MARION MILLS MILLER)

Sappho knows the story of Leda and the egg.
Edmonds (E. 97) reads a new text: "They say
that once upon a time Leda found hidden an
egg of hyacinthine hue." But I prefer the older,
better version, which O'Hara renders:

Once on a time
They say that Leda found
Beneath the thyme
An egg upon the ground.

Sappho makes a sarcastic reference to Leto and Niobe as very dear comrades (E. 140), and gives Niobe nine children of either sex (E. 168). She knows the love of the Moon for Endymion in the cave on Mt. Latmus (E. 167); she wrote about Theseus (E. 169), Prometheus (E. 170), Medea (E. 185), and Philomela and Procne, "the heavenly swallow, Pandion's daughter" (E. 122). Perhaps Sappho pictured the story of Hero and Leander (cf. p. 31). Stebbing changes the sex of Hero and makes a long poem on *Champion, Athlete, and Harpist*:

"Hero" of Gyaros; Hellas cannot forget his name.
The lovely, gallant youth, a paragon in women's eyes.

The divinities in Sappho are primarily Aphrodite, Peitho, Ares, Hecate, Hera, Hermes, Hephaestus, and the Muses. There is much reverence in the beautiful Hymn to Hera, the latter half of which Edmonds (E. 40) has so very tentatively restored on the hypothesis that this was written in Syracuse before Sappho embarked to return to Mytilene on hearing of the amnesty of Pittacus.

Sappho was not only the poet of ardent love, as we have seen, but the greatest composer of wedding-songs of antiquity, and much of such poetry in later days is nothing but a translation

[85]

or a transfusion of Sappho. Her *Epithalamia* were written for actual wedding ceremonies, but I cannot agree with a great German critic who says that they were not literary productions. I do not mean to say that she published these songs, for I believe that they were not collected into a ninth book until later days. We have already quoted what may be an introductory poem to the Epithalamies; perhaps even some of the other fragments which we have mentioned, such as that perfect weaving-song, which may reflect the awakening of love in the heart of the bride, and certainly the verses on the *Evening Star* (p. 64) belong to her Epithalamies. The wonderful new poem (E. 66) with its Homeric genitives and datives and its Homeric forms of words on the *Marriage of Hector and Andromache* could be used as a wedding-song at any wedding:

HOME–COMING OF HECTOR WITH HIS BRIDE

(Recitation for "*The Wedding Day*")

SUSTAINED *by sturdy limbs a herald came*
Swiftly to folk of Ida. Quick as flame
The rumor ran, ere he the tidings told,
Through wide-wayed Ilium that Hector bold

*And his fair bride Andromache, so dear
Already to the town for fame as peer
In beauty of the woman that with hate
They passed upon the street with eyes avert
(The Grecian Helen, whom, as seers assert,
Her name had doomed to be the torch of Troy —
'Destroyer'), and more dear because the joy
She was of Priam's most beloved son,
Were at the landing. All the people run
Out of the gates; the young men yoke their steeds
To chariots, and each his charges speeds,
With harness jingling, to be first, and bring
Hector and Hector's bride to Priam king.*

*And so like gods to Ilium they came
Attended by the people's wild acclaim,
Nor knew that even then across the sea
Sailed swift Achilles, born their bane to be:
To drag dead Hector round the walls of Troy,
And doom to slavery his wife and boy.*

(MARION MILLS MILLER)

I do not feel that this poem was cold and super-
ficial as Miss De Courten and some other
critics say, for to me it is a dignified and simple
epic narrative, like the messengers' speeches in
Greek tragedy, introduced into the midst of
lyrics. It is almost perfect and well worthy of
Sappho. It makes us realize that Sappho's

activity was broader than we had supposed and brings her nearer to her predecessors and successors. It is a unique example, hitherto unknown, of a lyric narrative with epic intonations, throwing new light on the history of the ancient wedding-songs.[96]

A rhetorician of the fourth century A.D., Himerius,[97] has an interesting passage which bears on Sappho's wedding-songs and helps us interpret the fragments which are preserved:

"So it is time for us, my children, since we are summoning our Muses to marriage-dance and marriage-love, to relax the graveness of our music, so that we may the better trip it with the maidens in honour of Aphrodite. How hard it is to find a tune gentle enough to please the Goddess, we may judge from the poets themselves, most of whom, though past masters in love-poetry, went as bravely to the description of Hera as any boy or girl, but when it came to the rites of Aphrodite, left the song for the lyre and the making of the epithalamy entirely to Sappho, who when the contests are over enters the chamber, weaves the bower, makes the bride-bed, gathers the maidens into the bride-chamber, and brings Aphrodite in her Grace-drawn car with a bevy of Loves to be her playfellows; and her she adorns with hyacinths about the hair, leaving all but what is parted by the brow to float free upon the wayward breeze, and them she decks with gold on wing and tress and makes to go on before the car and wave their torches on high."

(EDMONDS)

[88]

Himerius refers to the mock contests which were a part of the wedding ceremonies. There was always an *agon* or sham fight, as in Greek comedy, running through the hymenaeal, to be succeeded in many cases by a real fight afterwards. The wedding echoed with noise which suggested the conflicts of prehistoric days when brides were captives of bow and spear, and all sorts of characters figured in this drama of real life. There was place for satire and ridicule as well as for praise. Even in recent years I have witnessed in a neighboring island, "Scio's rocky isle," the semblance of predatory warfare which the Chians keep up during their bridal ceremonies. And in 1902 I attended a three days' Turkish wedding at Chiblak, near the site of ancient Troy. On that occasion the frequent shooting and fighting, which resulted even in injuries to Turks and Greeks, made the noisy ceremony seem like a battle. In Sappho's day, as to-day in the Orient, a wedding was not a brief benedictory reading by a clergyman. It was a long-drawn celebration, a prolonged process rather than a precise pronouncement, with torchlight processions, dance, and song.[98] All these features emerge very clearly in Sappho, where we can trace the whole ceremony

from the weaving of the bridal bower (*pastas* =
portico or bower in Himerius as cited above)
to the aubade song of the next morning. Here
is the charming song, sung, in the same metre as
the famous *Linus Song*, by the bridesmaids as
they led the bride to the bridegroom's bed,
proud of their island and of their Sappho: [99]

> Up with the rafters high,
> *Ho for the wedding!*
> Raise them high, ye joiners,
> *Ho for the wedding!*
> The bridegroom's as tall as Ares,
> *Ho for the wedding!*
> Far taller than a tall man,
> *Ho for the wedding!*
> Towering as the Lesbian poet
> *Ho for the wedding!*
> Over the poets of other lands,
> *Ho for the wedding!*
>
> (EDMONDS 148)

Then follows a kind of lyrical marriage drama,
the bridesmaids representing the tribe of the
bride, the youths the clan of the bridegroom,
in this respect foreshadowing Catullus' double
choir. The maidens answer the young men's
praise by chiding Hesperus, the evening star,
whose coming heralds the union. The young

men in turn reply with the famous words already quoted, to which the sequel probably was "even so bring home the bride to the bridegroom." We think of Edmund Spenser's *Prothalamion* and *Epithalamion* which have many of the motives of the Greek epithalamium, with their reference to Hesper, with their beautiful descriptions of bride and bridegroom. I quote the lines about Hymen, which is Sappho's Greek refrain, rendered by the word "wedding" in Edmonds' version:

Hymen, iö Hymen, they do shout;
That even to the heavens theyr shouting shrill
Doth reach, and all the firmament doth fill.

The men praise marriage bliss; the maidens, virginity (E. 152, "I shall be ever-maiden," E. 159, "Can it be that I still long for my virginity?"). The bride says, "Maidenhead, maidenhead, whither away?" and the reply is, "Where I must stay, bride, where I must stay" (E. 164) [100]; a wonderful example of the way in which Sappho treats abstractions and inanimate things (cf. also E. 80, "Up, my lute divine and make thyself a thing of speech"). Sappho is the first to use such a personification [101] and it recalls Théophile Gautier in his reverse appli-

cation in *Mademoiselle de Maupin*. At least
it is difficult to think of the young Gautier
independently conceiving the striking figure
that is so characteristic of the genius of the
Lesbian poetess. This is the Frenchman's passage. It describes the fair heroine going out
into the world dressed in masculine habili-
ments to test men's fidelity in love:

"And, as I rode away down the alley of chestnut
trees, all the puerilities of my girlhood ran along
by the roadside, blowing me farewell kisses from
the tips of their tapering fingers. And one little
spirit in white, in a clear, silvery voice, cried:
'Madeleine, where are you going? I am your virginity, dear, but you look so fierce in your boots
and hose, with your plumed hat and long sword,
that I am not sure whether I should go with you.'

"I replied: 'Go home, sweet thing, if you are
afraid. Water my flowers and care for my doves.
But in sooth you are wrong. You would be safer
with me in these garments of stout cloth than in
airy gauze. My boots prevent it being seen that
I have a little tempting foot; this sword is my
defense against dishonor; and the feather waving
in my hat is to frighten away all the nightingales
who would come and sing false love into my ear.'"

In amoebean or antiphonic hexameter verses
(E. 150 and 151), as exquisite as Heine's *Du
bist wie eine Blume*, the maidens liken the virgin

state to the unplucked pippin, the married woman to the hyacinth or columbine, with which Aphrodite is also adorned in the passage from Himerius. As Tucker says: "a band of girls mock the men with failure to win some dainty maiden, and the men reply with a taunt at the neglected bloom of the unprofitable virgin. Say the maids (Pl. 9):

> On the top of the topmost spray
>   The pippin blushes red,
> Forgot by the gatherers — nay!
>   Was it 'forgot' we said?
>   'Twas too far overhead!

Reply the men:

> The hyacinth so sweet
>   On the hills where the herdsmen go
> Is trampled 'neath their feet,
>   And its purple bloom laid low;

and there unhappily the record deserts us." These lovely lines are about as well known as anything of Sappho's, owing to Rossetti's adaptation in his *One Girl*, a title altered in 1881 to *Beauty*, which the reader can find in Wharton. In modern times, Maurice Thompson, Gamaliel Bradford, and others have been in-

fluenced by them, though often an un-Sapphic
touch not in Sappho's verses is given, as in
Bradford's *Topmost Bough:*

> Don't *you love me now,*
> After *I have set you*
> On *love's topmost bough;*
> God, *then I'll forget you.*

The bridegroom now bears off the bride while
the chorus of youths praise the bride and the
chorus of maidens the bridegroom:

> What *may I best compare,*
> Dear *groom, with thee?*
> A *slender sapling, ere*
> It *is a tree.*
>
> (EDMONDS)

But as to-day the bridegroom disappears in the
society column of the newspaper behind the
splendor of the elaborate description of the
bride's gown, so in Sappho the praise of the
bride is far sweeter than that of the bridegroom.
Recall the lines of Rossetti and these verses in
the metre of one of Catullus' *epithalamia:*

> Bride, *thy shape is all delight*
> And *thine eyes shine soft and bright,*
> O'er *thy fair cheek desire is shed*

[94]

And honor showered on thy head
From the Lady of Love in heaven.

(EDMONDS)

Congratulations were offered also to the bridegroom:

No other maiden lives to-day,
Bridegroom, such as thine.

(EDMONDS)

Himerius seems to be quoting such a song of greeting to bride and bridegroom: "Bride that teemest with rosy desires, bride the fairest ornament of the Queen of Paphos, hie thee to bed, hie thee to the couch whereon thou must sweetly sport in gentle wise with thy bridegroom. And may the Star of Eve lead thee full willingly to the place where thou shalt marvel at the silver-thronèd Lady of Wedlock" (Edmonds). Himerius also tells us that Sappho "brings Aphrodite in her Grace-drawn car with a bevy of Loves" to the wedding. And the joy of the earthly festival is repeated far up among the clouds of Olympus where the celestial feast is described (E. 146) in verses the lilt of which Professor Gildersleeve has thus reproduced in his unpublished version:

[95]

T*he mixing bowl yonder*
W*as filled with ambrosia,*
A*nd Hermes 'gan ladle*
T*he drink to the gods all;*
T*he gods all uplifted*
T*heir beakers and pour'd out*
L*ibations and utter'd*
F*air wishes for bridegroom,*
[F*or fair bride fair wishes.*]

Stebbing in his *Friends of Man* has the Gods descend to the modest hall wherein the marriage feast is spread.

A*ll the High Gods from Olympus, to bless the Two, descend.*

. . . .

B*y an ample bowl Hermes, deftest of cupbearers, stands,*
C*rowning the Gods' goblets from the full flagon in his hands.*

The function of what we Americans used to call the first groomsman, in the primitive times of wife-stealing, was to protect the bridegroom from pursuit and the name " best man " perpetuates the tradition. In the Greek wedding, where the passing and closing of the door was so essential a part of the ritual, he was the door-keeper, and

there was much bantering and chaffing at his
personal appearance on the part of the maidens,
who made much use of the same jokes which
have since been applied to the feet of maidens
of Chicago. The feet of the porter were put in
the laughing stocks somewhat after this fashion
(E. 154):

Full seven fathoms stretch the feet of the porter,
Full five ox-hides were used for his shoe-soles,
Ten stout cobblers were needed to make them,

(D. M. R.)

to which Edmonds would make the ingenious
but doubtful addition based on Synesius "[and
his father lived in other ways an honest life,
but claimed to be better born than Cecrops]."
The door is shut and the mocking subsides, as
all chant for the groom, "Happy bridegroom,
the marriage is accomplished, as you prayed it
should be, and the maiden you prayed for is
yours" (E. 155); and for the bride they sing,
"O beauteous one, O lovely one, thine it is to
sport with the rose-ankled Graces and Aphrodite the golden" (E. 157). If Edmonds' tenta-
tive restoration of the end of the first book of
1320 verses is correct, "the maidens spend all
the night at this door, singing of the love that is

between thee, thrice happy bridegroom, and a
bride whose breast is sweet as violets. But get
thee up and go when the dawn shall come, and
may great Hermes lead thy feet where thou
shalt find just so much ill-luck as we shall see
sleep to-night" (E. 47). Evidently the maidens
saw little sleep that night, but finally silence falls
and in the early dawn is heard the last song of
the serenaders: "Farewell the bride, farewell
the bridegroom" (E. 160, 162).

This chapter should not close without a mention of the epigrams. Many have been attributed to Sappho, but three especially (E. 143,
144, 145) have been included in most of the
translations. They are, however, written in
normal epic language without any essential
traces of Sappho's Aeolic dialect. One, which
Wilamowitz would date as late as 400 B.C.,
according to Edmonds was inscribed on the
base of a statue of a nameless infant, dedicated
to Artemis in gratitude for her birth by her
priestess-mother. I prefer the older interpretation:

Maidens, that pass my tomb with laughter sweet,
A voice unresting echoes at your feet;
Pause, and if any would my story seek,
Dumb as I am, these graven words will speak;

'Once in the vanished years it chanced to please
Arista, daughter of Hermocleides,
To dedicate my life in virgin bliss
To thee, revered of women, Artemis!
O Goddess, deign to bless my grandsire's line,
For Saon was a temple priest of thine;
And grant, O Queen, in thy benefic grace,
Unending fame and fortune to his race.'

(O'HARA's adaptation)

The epigram on the fisherman (E. 145) is most
unlike Sappho. Fawkes, Elton, Neaves, and
many a modern poet have put it into verse: [102]

Above the lowly grave of Pelagon,
Ill-fated fisher lad, Meniscus' son,
His father placed as sign of storm and strife
The weel and oar, memorial of his life.

(O'HARA)

The two elegiac couplets on *The Dust of Timas*,
who died before her wedding day, are rather flat
and hardly worthy of Sappho's genius (E. 144);
but if Edmonds' restoration of one of Sappho's
fragments as referring to Timas is correct (p. 60
above), it may be genuine and in that case one
of the very few surviving early metrical epitaphs.
I give you the recent rendering by one of our

best modern American poets, Edwin Arlington
Robinson:

> *This dust was Timas; and they say*
> *That almost on her wedding day*
> *She found her bridal home to be*
> *The dark house of Persephone.*
> *And many maidens, knowing then*
> *That she would not come back again,*
> *Unbound their curls; and all in tears,*
> *They cut them off with sharpened shears.*

V. SAPPHO IN ART

THE HIGH regard of the ancients and moderns for Sappho appears especially in art. In olden days she was honored in town-hall and library. Many a statue and bust of her was erected and she was one of the few historical characters who were painted on Greek vases, which even quote her verses. She was sculptured also in terra-cotta and bronze.[103] It is well established [104] that her image was engraved on coins of Eresus and Mytilene, — a unique honor in early Greek days. Many (Pl. 10, 11) in the British Museum, in Paris, and elsewhere [105] bear representations sometimes of her head on the obverse with the lyre on the reverse, and sometimes her full figure standing or sitting. They differ much in the manner of the arrangement of her coiffure, some even showing the hair covered by a kerchief, a fashion still prevalent in modern Lesbus. They may be traced back to different types. Those which bear her name date from Roman Imperial times. In general Furtwängler [106] is right in contending

[101]

that it was not the custom to honor distinguished persons in such a manner before the days of Alexander. But the beautiful head which appears on early Greek coins of Mytilene of the fifth and fourth centuries B.C. may easily be Sappho and not her patron Aphrodite, even in cases where the type is adapted to that of the goddess of love. The lyre on the reverse and the individual features which resemble some of the busts of Sappho point that way. The beautiful face on the old coins was copied from some statue, perhaps one that was even earlier than that of Silanion. Farnell well says: [107] "the later hero cults of Homer at Smyrna, Sappho at Lesbus, and Aristotle at Stageira reveal the deep conviction of the Hellenic spirit that science and art are divine powers." If the head on these Mytilenaean coins is really Sappho, it is a silent but eloquent testimony to the reverence her name acquired after her death and to the perfection of her living work.

The oldest possible representation of Sappho with which I am acquainted is an archaic terra-cotta relief from Melos in the British Museum.[108] It dates only a few years after Sappho's time, and though not inscribed it may represent Sappho and Alcaeus. Sappho appears as a slender lady of average height (not of short stature as Ovid says), dressed in a long Ionic woven tunic and wearing sandals. She sits with lyre in left hand and plectrum in right, and the bearded Alcaeus stands before her with bowl in left and extending his right hand. He seems to be expressing with a smile his admiration of her new poetry, so different from his own archaic measure. There is probably no reference, as in the case of the Munich vase from Sicily,[109] to the famous lines which we have quoted (p. 27). On this vase the names Sapho (so spelt) and Alcaeus are painted beside the tall and stately figures who appear with lyre and plectrum. Sappho seems to be rebuking with almost a pouting expression her fellow-townsman Alcaeus, who bows his head as she speaks to him the famous lines. This pictorial translation of her verses and other representations show her great popularity in Athens in the fifth century B.C. This Munich *psycter* or cooling mixing-bowl (Pl. 12) for wine may date as late as 460 B.C. and has been attributed to a fictitious lady painter of the Free Style by Hauser, but his attribution has not been generally accepted.[110] Furtwängler was probably right in connecting the vase with the Brygus painter.

[103]

My learned friend, the great Oxford expert on vases, Mr. J. D. Beazley writes me that very likely it was not by the Brygus painter himself, but surely in his manner. On an earlier vase, now in the Czartoryski collection in Cracow (Pl. 13), dating from the end of the sixth or the beginning of the fifth century B.C., according to Beazley a vase roughly related in style to the Nicoxenus painter, a contemporary of Euthymides, we have the earliest certain representation of Sappho.[111] She is a tall, draped figure with smiling countenance, walking to right and holding a seven-stringed lyre in her left hand and a plectrum in her right. She appears on only this one black-figured vase, which would seem to indicate that she did not become popular in Athens till long after her death, when red-figured vases were the vogue. The story of Solon adds testimony to the same effect, and probably a *corpus* or collection of her writings used by the later Alexandrian editions was in the book-stalls at Athens even in the last years of the sixth century. Otherwise it is difficult to account for her frequent portrayal on Attic red-figured vases. The lost Middleton vase,[112] (Pl. 14), probably of the South Italian (Lucanian) Style, shows Sappho, whose name is now thus spelt,

[104]

seated on a four-legged stool while a nude winged
Eros hastens towards her with a wreath. The
painter probably knew the poems of Sappho
which pictured Eros as bitter-sweet, and
Sappho's other word-pictures of the sorrows of
love, for he has labelled Eros "wretched." One
thinks of Horace's *querentem Sappho puellis de
popularibus*. Mr. Beazley, however, suspects
the inscription *talas*, and thinks that *kalos*
(beautiful) was written. It is greatly to be
hoped that the vase will soon be found again
so that we can have a rereading of the letters.
On the Michaelis vase in late Polygnotan style,[113]
which is in the Jatta collection at Ruvo in Italy
(Pl. 15), we possibly have an apotheosis of
Sappho. Aphrodite is painted with a cupid on
her right shoulder like the Aphrodite of the Parthenon frieze, judging the contest of Thamyris.
Near Apollo are three Muses, and near Thamyris
are four. Sappho is evidently leaning for support
on Aphrodite, receiving a little dove from a
little Eros, and is pictured as a Muse herself,
as in Plato's epigram. On another red-figured
vase [114] in private possession, Sappho is in the
midst of her pupils.

Several vases even show knowledge of her
writings. The most important is the hydria or

water-jar in Athens (Pl. 16), dating about 430
B.C.,[115] which Mr. Beazley would put in the group
of Polygnotus, somewhat in the style of the
Hector painter, though not by him. Sappho is
seated on a light-backed chair or *klismos*; she is
reading from a papyrus roll, while Nicopolis
behind holds a wreath over her head. Two
maidens stand in front, one, Callis, holding a
lyre. Scholars have long tried to make sense out
of the letters on the papyrus, and several, such
as Comparetti and Aly, have considered them
un-Sapphic; but Edmonds, the great English
expert on Sappho, has got a new reading for the
last word and thinks this is column 1 of a book
entitled *Winged Words*, a phrase borrowed from
Homer. The verses are an introductory poem
to Sappho's works with an invocation to the
Gods, after which follows the verse: "The
words I begin are words of air, but for all that,
good to hear." I do not feel that the solution is
satisfactory or Sapphic, and an examination of
the vase itself proves that Edmonds' reading will
not stand; but no one has yet made a better pro-
posal. On another vase, in the Louvre, attributed to Euphronius [116] we have an echo of Sappho in the words (E. 23), "I long and I yearn."
A beautiful fifth century cylix (Pl. 9) by the

erudite and versatile Sotades,[117] whose wonderful
signed terra-cotta horse, mounted by an Amazon,
has recently been brought to Boston from Meroe
in Egypt, pictures a girl on tiptoe trying to
pluck the sweet apple which is reddening on
the topmost bough. I have no doubt that
Sotades was illustrating Sappho's song.

Possibly on the so-called Steinhauser terra-
cotta fragment [118] the seated figure is Sappho;
she is nude above the waist and holds her lyre
in her right hand. She is looking into the air
enraptured and sublimely inspired.

Many vases have been interpreted as portray-
ing Sappho and Phaon,[119] but in every case there
is uncertainty about the interpretation. On
two beautiful vases (Pl. 4, 5), the hydria in Florence certainly by the Meidias painter himself,
and the crater in Palermo of the school of the
Meidias painter, the beautiful Phaon is definitely
pictured.[120] The inscription on the latter,
"Phaon is beautiful," leaves no doubt in the
matter. But the girl called Chryse or Philomele
is perhaps wrongly interpreted as Sappho.
These vases are probably older than the comedy
on *Phaon*, by Plato (not to be confused with the
philosopher). Phaon is painted as handsome;
all the girls are adorning themselves and making

love to him, but he has had too much attention
from the ladies and is sick of them (cf. p. 40
above). On another crater,[121] in Bologna (Pl. 17),
in style not far removed from the vase-painter
Polygnotus, Phaon appears seated at the oar
in a boat, about to take aboard the tall goddess,
who was to give him a perennial antidote against
old age.

Before we leave ancient painting we ought to
mention a picture of Sappho in a garb as a lutist
which the encyclopaedic Pliny assigns to Leon.[122]
We know nothing about him, but he was
probably one of the numerous second rate
artists of Hellenistic times. An epigram in the
Anthology and the Christian Father Tatian [123]
seem to have referred to this portrait. Several
Pompeian frescoes, and one from Herculaneum
representing a lady with a *stilus* about to write
her thoughts on a tablet, have been named
Sappho. Only in the case of one [124] do I feel
that there is any probability at all that Sappho
was meant, and in that one Alcaeus appears
standing by the side of the seated Lesbian
poetess (Pl. 18).

There must have been statues and busts of
Sappho, but so many have been called Sappho
without definite evidence that it is difficult to

know where to stop. We must always bear in mind that early Greek art in Sappho's day did not believe in realistic portraiture and that all representations of Sappho are "study heads," conceptions of later artists. The most famous statue mentioned in literature is that by Silanion, the Greek sculptor of the fourth century B.C., who was so noted for his Plato and Corinna.[125] We learn from Cicero's *Oration against Verres*[126] and from Tatian's *Complaint against the Greeks or Pagans* that this bronze statue, on the base of which Cicero was still able to read the epigram, stood in the prytaneum at Syracuse, perhaps a memorial of Sappho's sojourn in Sicily. Cicero tells us that it was stolen by Verres and praises it highly: "Could this work of Silanion, so perfect, so refined, so finished, be in fitter hands public or private than those of a man so refined and cultured as Verres? . . . And how sorely this stolen Sappho was missed is almost more than words can tell. Not only was the poetess exquisitely portrayed, but there was a world-famous Greek couplet inscribed upon the base . . . For the inscription on the empty base declares to-day what the statue was, thus proclaiming the theft" (Edmonds).

[109]

We know from literature of the existence of
two other later statues. We have spoken
(p. 34) of the epigram of Damocharis which
refers to a portrait of Sappho with bright eyes
and mixed expression of gaiety and graveness.
An epigram by Antipater [127] (p. 8) is thought to
come from a statue at Pergamum and since part
of an inscription found at Pergamum [128] mentions Alcaeus, it is a plausible conjecture that
the lost portion contained the name of Sappho.
This is probably the same bronze seated statue
which in the fifth century A.D. stood in the
gymnasium of Zeuxippus at Constantinople and
which is described by Christodorus in his
Greek Anthology: [129] "She seemed to be weaving a well-hymned song, concentrating her
thought on the silent Muses."

No full-size statue which we can certainly
identify as Sappho's has been preserved. The
seated lady in the Vatican holding a volume in
her left hand is hardly Sappho, and it is not safe
to call the standing lady with lyre in New York
in the Metropolitan Museum by her name.
It would be interesting to believe, as some do,
that the famous maiden of Anzio in the National
Museum in Rome was Sappho, but some
scholars of repute even go so far as to say that

it is not even a maiden but rather a boy. Others
say that a priestess, not a poetess, is portrayed.
After repeated examination of the original I
have no doubt of her sex and believe the statue
to be that of a poetess, but whether of Praxilla
or Sappho or some other cannot be definitely
stated. We have, however, many Roman busts
of different types [130] which have been conjectured
to represent Sappho. One type in all probability
is copied from Silanion, as it resembles closely
in the features of the face and the arrangement
of the hair, especially the little curls in front of
the face and in the covering of the head, the
portrait of Sappho on the early coins of Mytilene.
The best example of this type is the bust in the
Villa Albani in Rome (Pl. 19). It has the perfection, refinement, and finish to which Cicero
referred, and Sappho is "exquisitely portrayed."
In the Biscari collection at Catania, Sicily, there
is a Roman copy of a head meant to be inserted
in a bust or statue. It is so poorly finished that
it was probably placed in a niche or chapel to be
seen from a distance. The oval face is young
but placid and cold, a characteristic partly due
to the Roman copyist. With its corkscrew
curls and in other respects it is similar enough
to the busts in the Villa Albani and the Galleria

Geographica of the Vatican to be classed with them. If they represent Sappho, the Sicilian bust also does. If Rizzo is right that this is a muse or nymph, then a copy of Silanion's statue still remains to be found.

The so-called head of Sappho in the Pitti in Florence is of a different type, more dream-like, and may not be Sappho at all. More likely to represent Sappho are the busts in Oxford (Pl. 20) and the Vatican. Other busts about which there is considerable doubt are in Naples, in the Riccardi Palace, in the Uffizi at Florence, and there is a double herm in Madrid which has been called Sappho and Phaon. Of the so-called Phaon in Madrid, Amelung has recently found in the storcrooms of the Vatican a beautiful replica, and he has also discovered there another Sappho bust of the type on coins. In the summer of 1922 I photographed a bust, which is in the Borghese Palace, and I think that it may represent Sappho (Pl. 21). It resembles a colossal head from Smyrna in Constantinople, the bust in Naples, and the double bust in Madrid in its energetic and individualized features, such as the large nose and thick lips, and in the curl on the forehead beneath the middle of the fillet. Rizzo would trace the Naples bust back to about

420 B.C. and call it an ideal representation of a mortal or perhaps even a courtesan. But Sappho might easily have been represented in the type of a courtesan or even a muse. The large bronze bust in New York which has been published as a portrayal of Sappho can hardly represent the poetess, even if the bronze is genuine and has the sanction of great authorities such as Eisen,[131] Babelon, and André, since it resembles none of the known portraits of her. The Romans as well as the Greeks were undoubtedly very fond of statues of Sappho, and some day excavators will turn up for us more authenticated portraits. The recently discovered Roman stucco relief which we have already described (p. 42) shows what we may expect from future discoveries. Even such articles of every-day-use as scales have weights in the form of a Sappho head, such as that recently discovered.[132]

What we have said about the uncertainty of representations of Sappho in ancient sculpture applies equally to the portrait of her on gems. Cipollini has listed and illustrated many ancient and modern gems and miniatures, but even if those called ancient are forgeries or are from Renaissance times, the great number of them shows the unusual influence of Sappho on the glyptic art in precious stones.

After Roman days Sappho was often pictured and sculptured in various ideal ways.[133] Space fails us to discuss the almost endless works of later art influenced by her name and traditions; and it seems idle to detain the reader with a detailed catalogue. But to leave no doubt that Sappho has had a vast and powerful influence on art of all ages, I may mention some of the more important. During the last sixty years especially, sculpture has paid a frequent and international tribute to her. Now she is represented as sad and pensive, now meditating suicide, now about to make the fatal leap from the Leucadian rock as in Pietro Magni's Saffo (1866), now even as a corpse on the surface of the sea. Magni's statue (Pl. 22) was much admired during his lifetime and it reminds one of the Roman stucco relief, since it likewise represents Sappho, lyre in hand and with head wreathed, standing on the edge of the rock. She is holding back her skirts with her left hand and looking seriously at the waters below, with the intention of stepping off at the next moment. In 1878 the illustrious Lombard sculptor, Francesco Confalonieri, influenced it may be by the

Vatican Agrippina, made a seated statue which represents Sappho in profile with sad and bowed head, clasping her hands on her left side, her lyre abandoned on the floor. France did not approve of this statue because some years before Pradier also had sculptured a draped and dreaming Sappho who was seated on the Leucadian rock with bowed head and hands clasped about her raised crossed left leg, her lyre lying neglected on the rock (Pl. 23). Pradier had also sculptured a standing, draped Sappho with bowed head holding her lyre in her left hand, and supporting her right on an Ionic column on which rest the rolls of her divine poetry.

The great German sculptor Danneker, who was so fond of classical subjects and was the sculptor of the famous Ariadne, chiselled a charming marble statuette of Sappho (1796). The beautiful bas-relief in Greek style in the Vienna Volksgarten, which R. Weyr sculptured for the Grillparzer Monument, represents Sappho's farewell. She stands in drapery like that of the Erechtheum Caryatids. She is holding a lyre and kissing good-bye to a girl friend who gives her a last embrace. A shepherd kneels nearby and others in the background are recoiling in fear. She herself stands at the edge of the steps in front of Apollo's temple, and there is much other Greek architecture in this relief.

In France, Claude Ramey (1801) exhibited a seated statue; Duret (1806), a Sappho writing to Phaon; Beauvallet (1817), a bust; Diebolt (1848), a dying Sappho of noble and poetical expression. Other statues of Sappho were made and exhibited in the Salon by Laurent (1849), Grootaers (1852), Travaux (1852, now in the Louvre), Aizelin (1853, bronze), Loison (1859), Grabowski (1859), Clésinger (1859, three statues, "Sappho singing her last song, Seated on the Leucadian rock," "The youth of Sappho," and a polychrome statue), Robinet (1861), Doriot (1872), and Signora Maraini. In America, too, from the days of Story and Hezekiah Augur to the bronze doors of the new Detroit Public Library Sappho has been a subject for sculpture. Many are the busts which are inscribed to-day with the name of Sappho, such as that by A. Gennai in the possession of Mrs. W. B. Hill of Baltimore, or that by Sheldon.

In painting, though not often a subject for the greatest painters, Sappho was represented in Greek and Roman days and ever since right down to the most famous modern picture of her and her pupils by Alma Tadema, of which we have given a description above (p. 32). Several pictures, such as Titian's *Sacred and Profane Love*, have been supposed by great critics to represent Sappho, but it is difficult to agree with Poppelreuter that Titian really meant to paint a Naiad counselling Sappho, who is lamenting her love in the forest, to take the Leucadian leap.[134] In some cases fortunately the painters themselves have labelled them. Raphael is perhaps the greatest painter who pictured her. He brings her significantly in his *Parnassus* (Pl. 24) into juxtaposition with Petrarch, who dedicated four verses of his tenth eclogue to her (see p. 136). She is represented prominently to the left of the doorway, resting her left arm on it and holding in her left hand a papyrus roll with the name Sappho upon it. Other minor painters who have painted Sappho are Treshain (1683, "The Adventures of Sappho"), Ansiaux (1801), Ducis (1812), Vafflard (1819, "Sappho rescued from the water by a stranger"), Girodet (1828, a series of compositions from her first love affair to the legendary leap), Lafond (1831), Vien (1833, "Sappho playing the lyre," and "Sappho reciting to Phaon"), Chasseriau (1850), Chautard (1855), Agneni (1857, "Sappho rescued from the water by the Nereids"), Credès (1859),

Kauffmann (two beautiful pictures, "Sappho inspired by love" and "Sappho talking with Homer;" these like many of the other pictures were also engraved). Barrias painted a sleeping, nude Sappho, with her lyre by her side, and represents her perhaps repeating the words: "The silver moon is set; The Pleiades are gone; Half the long night is spent, and yet I lie alone" (Merivale). Other painters of Sappho are Fragonard, Gros, Devosge, Bartolazzi, Picou (1863), Loir (1864), Chifflart (1865), Bertrand (1867, "Death of Sappho"), Gastaldi (1873, "Sappho meditating suicide"), Gleyre ("Couch of Sappho"). Hector Leroux in his "School of Sappho" represents her standing in the atrium of a Roman house, with lyre in her left hand, on a platform inscribed with the name of the Lesbian Sappho, evidently giving instruction to her many friends and pupils who stand and sit in various postures in the audience.

This is only a partial list and could easily be extended, but enough has been said to show that a knowledge of the real Sappho and her writings and the legends connected with her will help one to be a sound and intelligent critic of much in the realm of art.

VI. SAPPHO'S INFLUENCE ON GREEK AND ROMAN LITERATURE

IF SAPPHO'S influence on art has been considerable, her place in literature has been far more remarkable. Nearly every thought in her fragments, which were known before the recent papyrus additions, has been borrowed or adapted by some ancient Greek or Roman poet or some modern poet in English, Italian, French, German, or modern Greek. Even the Spanish, Scandinavians, and Russians (p. 233) know her, though not so well acquainted with her as the authors of other nations. A very remarkable thing is that her writings have in all the ages been almost never unfavorably criticized from a literary point of view, no matter how her character was regarded. We have already, in giving a résumé of Sappho's writings, cited many an echo, many a translation, many a dilation or dilution, but have seen that the real flavor of Sappho's Greek cannot be transferred to any other language. In this and succeeding chapters, however, some of the names of writers who owe much to her will be brought together. She herself was original and coined many a new idea, many a new word, and perfected a new form of metre. Just as a modern poet, Tennyson for example, is indebted to his predecessors, Keats, Shelley, Shakespeare, for images and ideas, she was somewhat indebted in language and thought to Homer,[135] who filled the fancy of the Lesbians and was himself, probably, born at the neighboring Smyrna. She took little from Hesiod, although we find a few echoes of him which I cite in a note.[136] On the other hand, succeeding poets of the next hundred years seem to have taken little from her. Mimnermus probably knew the second ode, and his lines are included in the Corpus of Theognis.[137] If the fragment "Gold is Zeus' child, no moth nor worm devours it (E. 110)" is Sappho's and not originally written by Pindar himself, then Pindar took that idea from Sappho.[138] Herodotus tells the story of Rhodopis, and Plato, who would exclude poets from his ideal state, makes Socrates speak in the *Phaedrus* of the beautiful Sappho as one of the wise ancients, and he calls her the Tenth Muse in his famous epigram.

Aristotle, who refers to her three times, is the

first one definitely to quote her verses and that twice in the *Rhetoric* (E. 91, 119, and p. 159). Aristotle's pupil Theophrastus, who was also born in Eresus cites her (περὶ λέξεως, Mayer, 1910) as the representative of charm in all its forms. That essential element of charm is emphasized by Plutarch and by Demetrius, the rhetorician of the first century A.D., in his *Essay on Style*. Another pupil of Aristotle, Chamaeleon (310 B.C.), wrote a book about her.

Sappho's influence was not great in the field of Greek and Roman tragedy. Aeschylus and Sophocles betray no acquaintance with her, but Euripides was considerably affected by her verses on love. When he writes in *Electra* (l. 67), "I consider you a friend equal to the gods," he is thinking of the first verse of Sappho's second song. Plutarch cites Aristoxenus as saying that the tragedians learned the mixed Lydian mode from her. In comedy Aristophanes had a slight acquaintance with her, and he was thinking of Sappho's first hymn in his suffragette play *Lysistrata* (ll. 723 ff.), where a love-sick devotee of Aphrodite endeavors to escape from the Acropolis on the back of the sparrow, Aphrodite's bird. Epicrates dealt with Sappho in his comedy, *Anti-Laïs*, before the year 392 B.C.; and Athenaeus applies the words of Epicrates to himself:

*And all the songs that Sappho sang so sweetly,
Breathing of love, I know by heart completely.*

Sappho was the title of plays by six different Greek comedians, Ameipsias, Amphis, Antiphanes, Diphilus, Ephippus, and Timocles. Of those by Ameipsias and Amphis we have only a single word, and the fragments of the others throw little light on the question as to how much was taken from Sappho herself. To the plays of Plato, Menander, and Antiphanes on the legends of Phaon and the Leucadian Leap, we have already referred (p. 41).

In the Hellenistic Age, after the time of Alexander, Sappho was very popular. Clearchus, the Peripatetic philosopher (300 B.C.) drew on her for his *Treatise on Love Matters*.[139] In the third book of his *Biographies* Aristoxenus, a writer on music (320 B.C.), classes her among inventors as did Menaechmus of Sicyon in his treatise *On Artists*. He says that "her books were her companions."[140] The third century B.C. showed a serious interest in the Lesbians, and Theocritus has many imitations of Sappho in dialect,[141] metre, and content. In the second idyl Simaetha's description of her feelings is taken from Sappho. In the seventh idyl, the picture of the farm to which two friends walked out from Syracuse in order to attend a harvest home festival, Theocritus is imitating Sappho's Garden of the Nymphs, especially in ll. 135 ff.: "Close at hand the sacred water from the nymphs' own cave welled forth with murmurs musical" (Lang). Probably the eighteenth idyl on Helen and Menelaus borrowed much from Sappho, since the first lines seem to be cited as Sappho's by Himerius. Line 38, "O maid of beauty, maid of grace," is lifted bodily from Sappho. The twenty-eighth idyl on *A Distaff* undoubtedly employed Sappho as a model, and likewise the twenty-ninth and thirtieth idyls.

Callimachus (270 B.C.) in his first hymn (ll. 95 ff.) echoes the fragment which influenced Pindar (E. 100): "Wealth without virtue cannot make men happy, nor virtue without wealth, therefore grant both virtue and wealth." It was about the same time that a fellow townsman, Callias, interpreted her poems as well as those of Alcaeus. Apollonius of Rhodes (260 B.C.) knew her, and so did the *Lament for Bion*, which has been attributed doubtfully to

Moschus (150 B.C.): "Oh, Bion, Mytilene bewails thy song evermore instead of Sappho's" (III. 91). Bion (100 B.C.?) in his *Lament for Adonis* was probably influenced by Sappho's words about the dying Adonis (E. 103) and used in l. 44 the same word as Sappho did in E. 29. The philosopher Chrysippus (240 B.C.) mentions her (fr. 36, 69), as does Cicero's contemporary, the poet-philosopher Philodemus (60 B.C.). In fragment 57a he speaks of her, and in an epigram he uses as an "intelligence test" of an educated woman a knowledge of the poems of Sappho. Alexander the Sophist gave a university extension course of lectures on her poems. A little later in the Augustan Age the great literary critic and grammarian, Dionysius of Halicarnassus (20 B.C.), quotes the hymn to Aphrodite, and Strabo calls her a marvel. Living probably sometime in the first century A.D., the anonymous author of the *Treatise on the Sublime* quotes the second ode. A little later, about 85 A.D., the golden-tongued orator, Dio, cites her, and his contemporary Plutarch often refers to her, in his *Essay on Love*, 18; in his *Dinner-table Problems*, VII. 8, 2; in his *Moralia*, 243b, 622c, and 406a, where there is a comparison with the practice of *Paiderastia* of Socrates. Plutarch prefers Anacreon, but refers to at least four of the fragments which are preserved from Sappho (E. 2, 48, 71, 137).

Among the Romans Sappho was flattered abundantly, if imitation is the sincerest flattery. As Tucker says: "the most genuine lyric poet of Rome, Catullus, and its most skilful artificer of odes, Horace, both freely copied her. They did more than imitate; they plagiarised, they translated, sometimes almost word for word." The flattery does not begin until the time of Cicero, for Latin comedy, unlike Greek comedy, paid little heed to the Lesbian poetess. Cicero refers to Silanion's statue (p.109). Lucretius must have taken his description at second hand, perhaps from some medical source, if he did not take the verses of the second ode of Sappho direct as his model for his description of fear.[142] Catullus (84–54 B.C.),[143] who caught the Greek rhythm even better than Horace, translated the same ode in his famous fifty-first poem, addressed to Lesbia, and adapted the fragments on the hyacinth and the evening star in his *epithalamia*, the sixty-first and sixty-second songs in the Catullian collection. Probably in the sixty-second he is imitating a lost poem of Sappho. The verse of Sappho (E. 142), "I flutter like a child after her mother," referring perhaps to a wounded bird, has been used by Catullus in his well-known third poem, on the *Passer*, which probably also imitated a poem of Sappho.

In XI. 22–24, Catullus was perhaps thinking of Sappho's stricken hyacinth, although some rustic proverb may also have been in his mind:

> *Qui illius culpa cecidit velut prati*
> *Vltimi flos, praetereunte postquam*
>   *Tactus aratro est.*

> *Think not henceforth, thou, to recall Catullus'*
> *Love; thy own sin slew it, as on the meadow's*
> *Verge declines, un-gently beneath the ploughshare*
>   *Stricken, a flower.*

(ROBINSON ELLIS)

From these lines and not from Sappho herself, of whom there is no echo in Virgil, Virgil took his description of the dying Euryalus:

> *And like the purple flower the plough cuts down*
> *He droops and dies.*

(*Aeneid*, IX. 435)

We are reminded of Robert Burns' *To A Mountain Daisy:*

> *But now the share uptears thy bed,*
>   *And low thou lies!*

[126]

. . . .

Stern Ruin's ploughshare drives, elate,
    Full on thy bloom,
Till crushed beneath the furrow's weight,
    Shall be thy doom!

We refer on p. 9 to Catullus' allusion to Sappho in XXXV. 17.

In the age of Augustus, even if Virgil neglects Sappho, in Horace (65–8 B.C.) she is reborn. If Edmonds [144] is right in his analysis of a passage in Dio's *Corinthian Oration*, two fragments (E. 76, 77) of Sappho are incorporated there from a poem which Horace imitated in the same metre:

Exegi monumentum aere perennius.

Edmonds even goes so far as to suggest that Horace imitated not only the poem written by Sappho, but its position. For he thinks that this poem of Sappho was an epilogue to her collection; and Horace placed his imitation at the end of the third book, when he probably thought it would be his last. Horace seems to be adapting Sappho in the twelfth ode of the third book (see Landor's imitation, p. 202). He composed twenty-six or more odes in the

Sapphic metre, which he fitted to Italian measures, and he does them well, though in colder
Latin. In him

> *Still breathed the love, still lived the fire*
> *To which the Lesbian tuned her lyre.* [145]

He pictures her in Hades' home: [146]

> *Aeoliis fidibus querentem*
> *Sappho puellis de popularibus.*

The meaning is simply that she is "singing
plaintively (or complaining) about the girls of
her country," perhaps because they did not all
return her love, as Atthis deserted her for
Andromeda (E. 81); not that she complained
of her fellow-maidens for not loving Phaon.
Unconsciously Horace helped to defame Sappho's character, for the epithet *"mascula,"* in
the *Epistle* I. 19, 28, repeated by Ausonius,
Idyl, VI. 21, has led to gross abuse of Sappho's
good fame.[147] It has no relation to *mascu a
libido* and should be interpreted in the light of
Statius [148] as referring simply to the fact that
she was an imitator of the measures of Archilochus and the equal of men poets. Of elegiac
writers, Tibullus and Propertius (II. 8, 33) were
influenced only in a general way by the personal
and ardent poetry of Sappho's lyrics. Ovid in the

[128]

fifteenth epistle of the *Heroides* pictured Sappho
as a passionate and voluptuous *hetaera* who
could not win the love of the beautiful Phaon.
With passion she burns "as when through
ripened corn By driving winds the spreading
flames are borne," and seeks release and ease,
"from the raging seas." Ovid (43 B.C.–18 A.D.)
in this letter and also in the *Tristia* (II. 365,
Lesbia quid docuit Sappho nisi amare puellas)
completed the Roman defamation of Sappho's
good name begun by Horace, and so led the way
for the modern idea. From this disgrace she
has been rescued by Madame Anne Le Fèvre
Dacier (1681), by Welcker (1816), the bachelor
who loved Sappho's genius and who by his
chivalrous vindication made himself her knight,
and by Wilamowitz (1896), — her three great
defenders.

Seneca (*circa* 4 B.C.–65 A.D.) in his *Letters to
Lucilius* (88) quotes a book of the grammarian
Didymus on the question *Whether Sappho was
a prostitute*. In the Flavian period, Statius in
his miscellaneous poems, called *Silvae*, mentions
her: [148]

> *saltusque ingressa viriles*
> *Non formidata temeraria Leucade Sappho,*
> *Quosque alios dignata chelys.*

[129]

About the same time Martial (c. 40–104 A.D.) cites a poem [149] of Canius on Sappho: "Sappho the lover praised a poetess: more pure is Theophila, yet Sappho was not more learned" (Ker).

In the second century A.D. Sappho was especially popular. In the time of Hadrian, Dracon of Stratonicea wrote a book about Sappho's metres. In the days of Plutarch [150] the songs of Sappho were often sung at dinner parties. And Aulus Gellius (170 A.D.) in his *Attic Nights* [151] shows us that Sappho was all the rage in his day as in the time of Plutarch. It was the custom "after the chief courses were disposed of and the time was come for wine . . . to have delightful renderings of a number of the songs of Anacreon and Sappho." In the second century many writers on grammar, such as Apollonius Dyscolus and his son Herodian, Hephaestion (on metre), Demetrius (perhaps first century A.D.), Hermogenes, Maximus of Tyre, and Aristides (on rhetoric), Aelian, Pausanias, and Pollux quote Sappho abundantly. The great satirist Lucian (c. 120–c. 200 A.D.) calls her "the delicious glory of the Lesbians," [152] makes her the standard for ladies of learning who write poems, and has her contribute to one

of his pictures "the elegance of life." [153]   In
Loves (I, p. 905) he uses almost the very first
words of the second ode. That Galen, another
writer of the second century A.D., who knew not
only medicine but also the popularity of Sappho,
was speaking with authority on literature when
he said that Sappho was "*the* poetess," is shown
by the fact that most of the papyri with quotations from Sappho date from his time or from
the third century, the century when Athenaeus
and Philostratus, who cited much from Sappho,
were living.

In the fourth century Eusebius, Themistius,
and the Emperor Julian, as well as Himerius,
often quote her. Ausonius in *Idyl* VI says:

Et de nimboso saltum Leucate minatur
Mascula Lesbiacis Sappho peritura sagittis.

Claudian in his work on the *Marriage of
Honorius and Mary* (ll. 229–235) makes Mary
"never cease under her mother's guidance to
unroll the writers of Rome and Greece, all that
old Homer sang, or Thracian Orpheus, or that
Sappho set to music with Lesbian quill"
(Platnauer). In the fifth century the Christian
writer Synesius and that compiler of chresto-
mathies Stobaeus often quote from Sappho.

[131]

There is nothing to be gained by giving a long list of the writers on technical subjects to whom we owe so many fragments of Sappho not found on papyrus or parchment. Enough have been cited to prove that Sappho was much read in the first four and even the fifth centuries A.D. Himerius [154] especially proves her popularity in the fourth century, for he rewrites many of her songs in poetic prose and makes much use of Sapphic epithets and repetitions of words. The fragments (E. 68, 101) have influenced him in his *Orations*,[155] and in the *epithalamium*,[156] which he dedicated to his friend Severus in 354 A.D., Sappho's influence is very apparent (see above pp. 88 ff.). The bride is likened to an apple and the bridegroom to Achilles, although in the fragments preserved we have no Achilles but rather Ares.

The many epigrams [157] referring to Sappho, from Plato's couplet written in the fourth century B.C. to the time of Paul the Silentiary (who died 575 A.D.), some of which we have quoted above, bear out the testimony for Sappho's continuous influence through these thousand years; and now we can trace the reading of Sappho down to the seventh century, thanks to the finding in Egypt of two manuscripts of that century (E. 34, 82–86). Probably, however, Sappho's works were not much read even as early as the end of the sixth century. If so, Paul the Silentiary would never have written the epigram that appears in the Greek Anthology.[158] I give a literal translation: "Soft Sappho's kisses; soft the embraces of her snowy limbs, soft every part of her, but her soul is of unyielding adamant. For her love stops at her lips; the rest belongs to her virginity. And who could endure this? Perhaps one who has borne it, will endure the thirst of Tantalus easily." As Professor Gildersleeve [159] says: "Could Paulus have ever read anything of burning Sappho? We often envy the Byzantines their richer stores, but they seem to have been more familiar with Menander than with the early lyrists . . . Tell us, Pothos and Himeros, why has Paulus taken the name of Sappho in vain? We forgive him for playing with Theocritus' Galatea but he ought to have let Sappho sleep alone." Perhaps Paulus had heard of the question debated in school and society ever since the days of Didymus; and so he came to her defence with an interesting compromise on her tantalizing chastity.

VII. SAPPHO IN THE MIDDLE AGES AND THE RENAISSANCE

HOW LONG after the seventh century Sappho was read we cannot say, but in mediaeval days men were either entirely ignorant of her or had erroneous ideas. By the ninth century she seems to have become almost unknown, otherwise the critic and compiler Photius [160] would have preserved some of her works. He refers only to the tradition of her love for Phaon and the Leucadian Leap, and to the hypothesis that she was different from Sappho the courtesan, as she had been branded by that father of the church, Tatian (about 140 A.D.), who called her a female harlot, love-mad, γύναιον πορνικὸν ἐρωτομανές. That idea undoubtedly led to the burning of her books, according to Cardan, under Gregory Nazianzen, about 380 A.D. According to Scaliger, the burning took place in Constantinople and Rome in 1073. In any case, no manuscript has survived in Europe; and it is strange that now not even her legendary adventures with Phaon appear in the popular literature. The *Etymologicum Magnum* (1000 A.D.?) mentions her only five times, but in that way preserves for us five fragments. After the time of that lexicon and Suidas, the mediaeval encyclopaedias and the *Speculum Historiale* of Vincent de Beauvais of the thirteenth century make no mention of her, though they cite many another Greek poet. Georgius Cedrenus (1015 A.D.?), a Greek monk, who in his *Compendium Historiarum* said that she was "the first of the Muses," is about the only one of this time who notices her. Anna Comnena,[161] daughter of the Emperor Comnenus I, quotes as Sappho's the verses supposed to be addressed to Sappho by Alcaeus (E. 119). And the archbishop Eustathius preserves a few fragments. Dante makes no reference to her, unless possibly very faintly in the verse "le muse lattar più ch' altri mai." Boccaccio (1313–1375), who seems to have been forgotten by modern writers on Sappho, includes her among his *Delle Donne Famose*, "ma confortata da più caldo fervore d'animo (i suoi versi sono famosi) . . . e certamente non sono più famose che la sua corona le corone dei re, nè le mitre de' sacerdoti, nè le lauree de' trionfanti." Petrarch

(1304–1374) mentions Sappho in his *Triumph of Love* (IV. 25): [162]

> *Una giovane Greca a paro a paro*
> *Coi nobili poeti già cantando*
> *Ed aveva un suo stil leggiadro e raro.*

In his Tenth Eclogue he dedicated four verses to her:

> *Altera solliciti laqueos cantabit amoris*
> *Docta puella, choris doctorum immiata virorum*
> *Cinnameus roseo calamus cui semper ab ore*
> *Pendulus et dulces mulcebant astra querelae.*

Petrarch's friend, Domenico di Bandino of Arezzo (1340–c. 1415), professor at Bologna, gave her a brief article in his encyclopaedic *Fons Memorabilium Universi*. The other commentators on Petrarch ignore her. Giorgio Merula (1424–1494), Poliziano's adversary, accepts the whole Ovidian legend as historical fact and even adds a new item to Sappho's life by giving her a son Didas by her wealthy Andrian husband, Cercylas.

THE RENAISSANCE. There was now a second "floruit" of Sappho's fame, but like her previous popularity among the Romans the second renaissance was not favorable to Sappho, and there was no true understanding of the historical

Sappho. It was in the fifteenth century that Ovid's perverse epistle was discovered and from that time on it biased all Sapphic literature. The great humanist Poliziano knew her slightly and has left a Latin version of the epigram on Timas. Domizio Calderini (1447–1477), the learned though not overcritical humanist, based his little knowledge of Sappho on an uncritical use of Suidas. He even falsified Horace's *querentem* by forging in its place *gaudentem*, and transformed Sappho from the leader of a sacred sorority into a tribade [163] or lover of her pupils, even of the famous poetess Erinna. The result was that the great injustice done Sappho by Horace and especially by Ovid was much aggravated. Thanks to Tatian and Calderini, working at different times and in different fields, Sappho was even more misjudged in the seventeenth century. It would be idle to cite the many authors who mention or malign her but who give us little material of literary importance: Giraldi (1489–1552), Ludovico di Castelvetro (1505–1571), Giorgio Carraria (1514 A.D.), Iacopo Filippo Pellenagra (1517 A.D.), Francesco Anguillac (1572), who well renders the second ode, "Parmi quell'uomo equale essere à i Dei," Lorenzo Crasso (1625?), Ugo Foscolo (1776–

1827), and many another.[164] One needs only to
read the long account with many references in
the famous *Dictionnaire historique et critique*
(1696) by that learned compiler, Pierre Bayle
(1647–1706), who because of his scepticism
lost his professorship of philosophy three years
before (1693). In his ignorance he assumed
that Sappho must have been bad and repeated
the usual errors about her. I quote what he
says ironically with regard to the charity of
Madame Dacier: "charité de Mlle Le Fèvre
qui a tachè pour l'honneur de Sappho de rendre
le fait incertain; mai je la crois trop raison-
nable pour se fâcher que nous en croyons nos
propres yeux." Anne Le Fèvre [165] in 1681 had
made the first real defense of Sappho's character, long before Wilhelm Heinse's *Ardinghello*,
and one hundred and thirty-five years before
Johannes Friedrich Welcker,[166] who so influenced
Goethe and Comparetti and Wilamowitz.

VIII. SAPPHO IN ITALY IN THE 18TH AND 19TH CENTURIES

D URING the eighteenth and nineteenth centuries Sappho was rehabilitated and countless works of literature and art show her influence. Though the old perverse idea pervades all forms of literature and art in many insidious ways and Sappho loses her real personality and becomes a heroine of Romance, and although the legends connected with her are given a prominent place in the sunlight, yet even this proves her great potentiality in modern times.

The romantic Giacomo Leopardi (1798–1837), who translated passages from the *Odyssey* and wrote an interesting essay on the *Popular Errors of the Ancients*, composed also a *Last Song of Sappho*. In this poem, drawn from Ovid, he has given the modern reader a strong impression for better or worse of the stormy and passionate soul of the great poetess. As in his *Brutus*, Leopardi is giving his own views of life, which are biased by his physical affliction;

but he blends his sorrow with that of nature and rises, especially in the third stanza, almost to the heights attained by Aeschylus in his *Prometheus*. He ends his song with beautiful mysterious pathos:

> *Placida notte, e verecondo raggio*
> *Della cadente luna . . .*
>
> . . . .
>
> *Bello il tuo manto, o divo cielo; e bella*
> *Sei tu, rorida terra. Ahi di cotesta*
> *Infinita beltà parte nessuna*
> *Alla misera Saffo i numi e l' empia*
> *Sorte non fenno.*

> *Thou peaceful night, thou chaste and silver ray*
> *Of the declining Moon;*
>
> . . . .
>
> *Fair is thy sight, O sky divine, and fair*
> *Art thou, O dewy earth! Alas, of all*
> *This beauty infinite, no slightest part*
> *To wretched Sappho did the Gods or Fate*
> *Inexorable give . . .*
>
> (F. H. Cliffe)

One is reminded of Sappho's silver moon in Leopardi's calm first lines, and also of Sappho's autumn fragment in the lines " where in shade Of drooping willows doth a liquid stream

Display its pure and crystal course. . . ."
Leopardi also translated the famous midnight
song (p. 78) and imitated the third fragment in
La Impazienza. Carducci's (1888) comment on
Leopardi is worth quoting: "la poetessa di
Lesbo non fu nè brutta nè infelice come il Leopardi l'accolse a imagine sua da una tarda
tradizione, e che della bellezza e dell'amore
intese gustò, e cantò più non potesse il Leopardi." Leopardi believed in two Sapphos, as
did Zannoni (1822), following the judgment
of Visconti. About 1793, Pagnini (Pilenejo),
wishing to praise Teresa Bandettini Landucci,
likened her to Sappho in genius but not in
habit:

> Te *rediviva Saffo ognuno estima*
>   *Pari d'ingegno, e d'arte a quella prima:*
> Ma *per costumi e voglie in tutto sei*
>   (*Vanto maggior*) *dissimile da lei!*

Parini about 1777 dedicated an ode to Lady
Pellegrina Amoretti d'Oneglia on her graduation
from the University of Padua, *La Laurea,* in
which he said that if instead of studying law she
had given herself to literature she would have
been the equal of Sappho. In 1782 Verri pub-
blished *Le Avventure di Saffo,* in which there is a

paraphrase of the second ode. This romance was written in good literary style and had some fine thoughts and considerable Greek atmosphere. It went through more than a dozen editions, and was twice translated into French. In 1787 Parini celebrated the seductive qualities of a Venetian Signora Cecilia Tron in a poem of which I quote the first two stanzas:

> Che più dalla vivace
>   Mente, lampi scoppiavano
>   Di poetica face,
>   Che tali mai non arsero
>   L'amica di Faon;

> Nè quando al coro intento
>   Delle fanciulle lesbie
>   L'errante violento
>   Per le midolla fervide
>   Amoroso velen;

. . . . . .

One evening in 1827, as the story goes, the great Manzoni in the presence of Lamartine called La Palli, the happy-hearted Italian poetess, a "Saffo novella." Eurica Dionigi was called the "Saffo Lazia," and Anassilide was named "Saffo campestre" by the inhabitants on the Piave. Their verses, however, fall far short of the real

Sappho. In 1857 Giovanni Meli published *La Morti di Saffu;* and many another Italian writer has published poems in her honor, Gemma, Cipolla, Botti, etc.

Tragedies on the subject of Sappho in Italy have been few, among others those of Luigi Scevola (1815) and Salvatore Cammarono (1842); that of Leopoldo Marenco (1880) pictured Sappho as one of the Furies who was rejected by Phaon when he became enamored of another woman. Giovanni Pacini (Naples, 1840) first produced an opera on the theme, but changed the figure of Phaon to one who fell in love with Sappho and became jealous of Alcaeus, but was ready to die with him.

In recent years Carducci, in his *Primavere Elleniche*, makes Sappho and Alcaeus follow Apollo across the Aegean in a boat drawn by two white swans:

> D'INTORNO *girano come in leggera*
> D*anza le Cicladi patria de' l nume,*
> D*a lungi plaudono Cipro e Citera*
>   C*on bianche spume.*

> E *un lieve il séguita pe' l grande Egeo*
> *Legno, a purpuree vele, canoro:*
> *Armato règgelo per l' onde Alceo*
>   D*a' l plettro d' oro.*

Saffo da' l candido petto anelante
A l'aura ambrosia che da' l dio vola,
Da' l riso morbido, da l' ondeggiante
 Crin di viola,

In mezzo assidesi.

The influence of Sappho on Italian literature
is also seen in the many Italian translations of
some or all of the fragments; Cappone (1670),
Rogati (1783), Pilenejo (1793), Broglio d'Ajano
(1804), Leopardi (1816), Benedetti da Cortona
(1819), Foscolo (1822), Milani (1824), Zanotto
(1844), Jacopo d'Oria (1845), Nievo (1858),
Viani (1858), Bustelli (1863), Canini (1885),
and others have translated the famous folk-song
(see p. 78). Giovambattista Possevini (1565),
Francesco Anguilla (1572), Pinelli (1639), Cappone (1670), Corsini (1700), Conti (1739), Verre
(1780), Pindemonte (1781), Rogati (1783),
Vincenzo Imperiale (1784), Pilenejo (1793),
Tommaseo (1827), Comparetti (1876), Ardiz-
zone (1876), Fraccaroli (1878), Ambrosoli (1878),
Gemma (1879), Cavallotti (1883), De Guberna-
tis (1883), Canini (1885) have translated the
Hymn to Aphrodite. Rogati (1783), Gori
(1801), Montalti (1804), Broglio d'Ajano (1804),
Sabbione (1817), Venini (1818), Caselli (1819),

Foscolo (1823), Milani (1824), Costa (1825),
Accio (1830), Monti (1832), Leone (1843),
Nievo (1858), Canna (1871), Fraccaroli (1878),
Canini (1885) have translated or adapted the
second ode. D'Ajano (1804) gave the first complete version of all the old fragments, and in
1863 Bustelli did likewise, — neither of a high
order of merit. In 1890 Cipollini published his
verse translation of the first two odes and of
the fragment about the Pleiades, which his
brother set to music. The latest translation I
have seen is by Latini (1914) and it is an excellent piece of work. Italy has had for the last
hundred or more years a high regard for Sappho.
Cipolla, thinking perhaps of Meleager's comparison of Sappho's poems to roses, says:

> Ma i fior più belli
> Eran, Saffo, i tuoi canti, e ben sapevi
> Destinato a durar presso i futuri,
> Tra i più cari, il gentil nome di Saffo.

And Zanotto says:

> Le corde Lesbie risuonar d'amore
> Per te, donna gentil, vanto di Grecia;
> Et il tuo lamento ancor discende al cuore.

Many of the fragments besides those mentioned have been translated into Italian or

imitated by Italian writers, as for example
Zanella's famous imitation, *A donna ignorante:*

> *Tutta il sepolcro di accorrà: memoria*
> *Non fia che di te resti,*
> *Perchè le rose, del bel colle Aonio*
> *Le rose, non cogliesti:*
> *Tu senza nome scendarai dell'Erebo*
> *A'tenebrosi porti,*
> *E fatua larva fra le larve ignobili*
> *Vagolerai dei morti.*

Montalti (1804) imitated the fragment on virginity (p. 91), adding, however, much material of his own; and D'Oria (1845) expanded
Sappho's ten words on the evening star into:

> ESPERO *amabile,*
> *Tu sempre apporti*
> *A noi vivissime*
> *Gioie e conforti.*
>
> *Tu splendi, e subito*
> *Le tazze, piene*
> *Di licor, vuotansi*
> *A liete cene.*
>
> *Gli armenti all'umile*
> *Ovil riduce*
> *La soavissima*
> *Tua bianca luce;*

E *rende al tenero*
  Seno di quella,
  Ond'ebbe il nascere,
  L*a pastorella.*

Zanella (1887) says in his *Volo in Ellade*, which Cipollini quotes at length, that it is sweet to

S*alutar le riviere a cui fedele*
  L'eco dell'Ellesponto ancor ripete
  L'ardente inno di Saffo e le querele.

There is not space to speak further of Sappho's influence in Italy; we have said enough to show that Italian poetry has many echoes of Sappho and that Italy still takes an interest in the Lesbian lyrist. Ada Negri with her fiery pictures of passion is to-day called the modern Italian Sappho.

IX. SAPPHO IN LATIN TRANS-
LATIONS, IN SPANISH, AND
IN GERMAN

WE HAVE spoken of Sappho's influence on the ancient Latin authors
and especially of Catullus' translation and elaboration of the second ode. Horace
also may have translated whole odes, but we
have only Catullus' preserved. In later days
many of the editions of Athenaeus, Dionysius,
Pseudo-Longinus, Hephaestion, and of the
Anthology included Latin versions, and many
other writers have Latinized the fragments of
Sappho, especially Ausonius, Stephanus, Thomas
Venatorius, Lubinus, Poliziano, and Thomas
Moore. One of Moore's two versions of Plato's
epigram is quoted here:

Musas esse novem referunt, sed prorsus aberrant.
Lesbia jam Sappho Pieriis est decima.

Among the Latin translators of the odes have
been Elias Andreas, Simone Bircovio, Professor
Le Fèvre (Tanaquillus Faber), Zacharias Pearce,

Valentini, Barbagallo and Allucci, Ambrocio, Emilio Porto and Birkow, etc. Gorsse, A. Stace, Vossius, and Henri Etienne and others have rendered the second ode into Latin.

SPANISH. In Spain in 1794 there was a translation of Sappho and many other Greek lyric poets into Castilian verse by D. Jos. y D. Bernabé Canga Arguelles; and in 1832 appeared a prose and verse translation of Anacreon, Sappho, and Tyrtaeus by D. Jose del Castilla y Ayensa. Recently in Paris (1913) has been printed a modern Spanish version by T. Meabe. But in general Sappho has had but little influence on Spanish and German literatures, as compared with her great effect on Italian, French, and English. Mention, however, must not be omitted of the account of Sappho by A. Fernandez Merino. It is written in Spanish and discusses many of the Sapphic problems, giving full references.

GERMAN. In 1710 Philander von der Linde translated the second ode, and in 1732 Hudemann translated a few of the fragments, and there were good German editions of all Sappho's fragments as early as the careful one by Christian Wolf (1734). In 1744 appeared Neukirch's translation of the first two odes, and in 1746

Götz published his translation in rhymeless
verse. In the same year appeared Stählin's
translations. In 1764 "the German Sappho,"
Die Karshin, mentions Sappho five or six times
and Phaon, but has no direct echoes. In 1776
Meinecke put Sappho into verse; in 1782 Ram-
ler; in 1783 Günther Wahl. In 1787 verse
translations were published at Berlin and Lie-
bau, and in 1793 Conz published his translation
of the fragment, *To an Ignorant Girl*. In 1809
Friedrich Gottlieb Born edited an edition for
schools; in the same year C. Braun translated
the fragments; in 1810 Volger published his
very important and rare edition with commen-
tary and musical schemes. He was soon followed by Welcker's defense (1816), which
Goethe mentions four times. But Sappho's
poetry remained a closed book to Goethe.[166]
There were many succeeding editions or translations: Degen (1821), Neue (1827), Brockhausen's
verse imitations (1827), Richter (1833), Jäger
(1836), Gerhard's free rendering for German student songs (1847), Köchly (1851), Hartung
(1857), Weise (1878), Theodor Bergk's great
edition of 1882 reprinted in 1914; Schultz-
Geffcken's *Altgriechische Lyrik im deutschen
Reim* (1895), Stowasser, *Griechenlyrik in deutsche*

Verse übertragen (1910); and Wilamowitz, *Sappho und Simonides* (1913). There is a good German account of Sappho by Paul Brandt in his *Sappho, ein Lebensbild aus den Frühlingstagen altgriechischer Dichtung* (1905). In *Griechische Lyrik* (1920) Erich Bethe in a good chapter on Sappho translates into rhymed verse the first two odes and several of the fragments (E. 99, 119, 135, 114, 54, 71, as well as the new papyrus fragments E. 83, 149, 150, 148, 154).

I can quote here only the new fragment 83:

.   .   .   .

> *Weinend hat sie Abschied genommen,*
> *Immer wieder sprach sie so:*
> *'Hartes, Sappho, muss ich leiden,*
> *Muss dich lassen, muss nun scheiden.'*
> *Und ich hab zu ihr gesprochen:*
> *'Lebe wohl und denke mein!*
> *Wisse, dass dich treu geleite*
> *Meine Liebe in die Weite!'*
>
> *Denn stets werde ich gedenken,*
> *Auch wenn du es einst vergisst,*
> *Wieviel Schönes wir genossen,*
> *Wie du oft um schlanke Sprossen*
>
> *Veilchen wandest, Rosen bandest*
> *Und du mich damit bekränzt,*

[151]

*Und die duft'gen Purpurblüten
Deinen zarten Hals umglühten . . .*

· · · · · · · ·

There are only a few distinct cases of Sappho's influence on the great German poets, and so I limit myself to comparing Grillparzer's melo-dramatic adaptation of the Aphrodite ode with the beautiful rendering by the German lyric poet of modern times, Geibel, who as a tutor in Athens learned to love Lesbian lyrics and Greek literature, though he could not reproduce the wonderful soft sound of the Aeolic Greek:

GOLDEN-THRONENDE *Aphrodite,
Listenersinnende Tochter des Zeus,
Nicht mit Angst und Sorgen belaste,
Hocherhabne! dies pochende Herz!*

*Sondern komm, wenn jemals dir lieblich
Meiner Leier Saiten getönt,
Deren Klängen du öfters lauschtest,
Verlassend des Vaters goldenes Haus.*

*Du bespanntest den schimmernden Wagen,
Und deiner Sperlinge fröhliches Paar,
Munter schwingend die schwärzlichen Flügel,
Trug dich vom Himmel zur Erde herab.*

*Und du kamst; mit lieblichem Lächeln,
Göttliche! auf der unsterblichen Stirn,*

[152]

Fragtest du, was die Klagende quäle,
Warum erschalle der Flehenden Ruf?

Was das schwärmende Herz begehre,
Wen sich sehne die klopfende Brust
Sanft zu bestricken im Netz der Liebe;
'Wer ist's, Sappho, der dich verletzt?

Flieht er dich jetzt, bald wird er dir folgen;
Verschmäht er Geschenke, er gibt sie noch selbst,
Liebt er dich nicht, gar bald wird er lieben,
Folgsam gehorchend jeglichem Wink!'

Komm auch jetzt und löse den Kummer,
Der mir lastend den Busen beengt,
Hilf mir erringen, nach was ich ringe,
Sei mir Gefährtin im lieblichen Streit!

(GRILLPARZER)

DIE du thronst auf Blumen, o schaumgeborne
Tochter Zeus', listsinnende, hör' mich rufen,
Nicht in Schmach und bitterer Qual, o Göttin,
 Lass mich erliegen.

Sondern huldvoll neige dich mir, wenn jemals
Du mein Flehn willfährigen Ohrs vernommen,
Wenn du je, zur Hilfe bereit, des Vaters
 Halle verlassen.

Raschen Flugs auf goldenem Wagen zog dich
Durch die Luft dein Taubengespann, und abwärts

[153]

Floss von ihm der Fittiche Schatten dunkelnd
    Über den Erdgrund.

So dem Blitz gleich, stiegst du herab und fragtest,
Sel'ge, mit unsterblichem Antlitz lächelnd:
'Welch ein Gram verzehrt dir das Herz, warum doch
    Riefst du mich, Sappho?

Was beklemmt mit sehnlicher Pein so stürmisch
Dir die Brust? Wen soll ich ins Netz dir schmeicheln?
Welchem Liebling schmelzen den Sinn? Wer wagt es,
    Deiner zu spotten?

Flieht er: wohl, so soll er dich bald verfolgen;
Wehrt er stolz der Gabe, so soll er geben;
Liebt er nicht, bald soll er für dich entbrennen,
    Selbst ein Verschmähter.'

Komm denn, komm auch heute, den Gram zu lösen!
Was so heiss mein Busen ersehnt, o lass es
Mich empfahn, Holdselige, sei du selbst mir
    Bundesgenossin!

                                        (GEIBEL)

In 1793, Franz von Kleist at the age of twenty-four had written a tragedy *Sappho*, a typical eighteenth century play of intrigue, an immature performance, however, lacking in clear portrayals of character and in dramatic development. In 1816 F. W. Gubitz had published an unimportant monodrama *Sappho*, which was almost a caricature of what a dramatic work of art should be. In these dramas there was little of the real Sappho, but the case is different with Grillparzer's *Sappho*, which was given April 21, 1818, in Vienna with great success. Some of the motives of von Kleist reappear in Grillparzer, and there are resemblances in language and thought. He may have used Amalie vom Imhoff's *Die Schwestern von Lesbos* (1801), where there is a reference to the Leucadian Leap. But he rises to higher heights, and if he did use the above authors, their "crude ore," as one critic has expressed it, "yields pure gold." Grillparzer tells us himself in his autobiography [167] how he conceived the idea of the drama. On June 29, 1817, he was strolling along the banks of the Danube when at the entrance to the Prater, the great park of Vienna, he met Dr. Joël, who remarked that Weigel, the orchestra-leader, wanted a libretto. Dr. Joël stated that Sappho would be a good subject, and Grillparzer immediately replied that it certainly would make a good tragedy. They parted company, and Grillparzer walked deep into the Prater, and when he returned home late in the evening the plan of Sappho was complete. The next day he went to the Imperial Library and secured a copy of the extant fragments of Sappho, in which he found one of the two complete poems, which is addressed to the goddess of love, entirely suited to his purpose. He translated it at once, and the very next morning began work on the drama. The spirit of the play is German, not Greek, and takes some motives from Goethe's *Tasso*. But Sappho is depicted as a woman rather than a poetess, and the story of the tragedy is really that of an unhappy woman disappointed in love. While it is a genuine love-tragedy, it also portrays the hard lot of the poet and the struggle between art and life even more vigorously than Goethe's *Tasso* did. At the very beginning of the play Sappho has been crowned with the wreath of victory at the Olympic games and meets Phaon, who is represented as only slightly younger. Carried away by her triumph, he throws himself into her arms, only to spurn her later. To Phaon she sings (Act I, vi) Sappho's hymn to Aphrodite, which we have just quoted, with a few changes to adapt it to the situation. Of course there were no such contests at Olympia in Sappho's day, and Sappho's victory is a pure invention. Neither was the original hymn addressed to Phaon, nor did the usual legend

say that Sappho cast herself from a Lesbian cliff;
but Grillparzer must preserve the three unities,
and such dramatic licenses and many an-
achronisms, such as the mention of Croesus who
lived after Sappho's time, are permissible to a
master of dramatic technique. What interests
us is that Grillparzer actually studied Sappho's
fragments and was much assisted by them.
In Act I, lines 173 ff., he seems to be referring to
the Adonis fragments, including the one on the
loneliness of midnight, and to the verses which
name Andromeda and Atthis:

> *vom schönen Jüngling,*
> *Der Liebesgöttin liebeglüh'nden Sang,*
> *Die Klage einsam hingewachter Nacht,*
> *Von Andromedens und von Atthis' Spielen.*

The fragment (E. 74) is echoed in lines 671–2:

Denn, wenn auch heftig manchmal, rasch und bitter,
Doch gut ist Sappho, wahrlich lieb und gut.

While Grillparzer is one of the few German
poets who has imitated the content of Sappho's
songs, many have tried the Sapphic strophe
with success, especially Wilbrandt in the Adonis
song, in *Der Meister von Palmyra:*

Also will's der ewige Zeus; du musst nun
Niedersteigen unter die blüh'nde Erde,
Musst die dunkle Persephoneia küssen,
Schöner Adonis.

Many a German novel refers to Sappho, but without any special knowledge of her fragments. One of the most interesting, which adapts with many changes the Rhodopis story, has been translated into English, *An Egyptian Princess*, by George Ebers (A. L. Burt Co., New York, second German edition 1868). Here Charaxus actually marries Rhodopis and names their child Cleïs, who in turn has a child Sappho whose love-scenes with Bartja make up most of the novel.

"Alcaeus, the greatest poet of his day, and Charaxus, the brother of that Sappho whose odes it was our Solon's last wish to learn by heart, came here to Naukratis, which had already long been the flourishing center of commercial communication between Egypt and the rest of the world. Charaxus saw Rhodopis, and soon loved her so passionately that he gave an immense sum to secure her from the mercenary Xanthus, who was on the point of returning with her to his own country; Sappho wrote some biting verses, derisive of her brother and his purchase, but Alcaeus on the other hand, approved, and gave expression to this feeling in glowing songs on the charms of Rhodopis. And now Sappho's brother, who had till then remained undistinguished among the many strangers at Naukratis, became a noted man through Rhodopis. His house was soon the center of attraction to all foreigners, by whom she was overwhelmed with gifts. The king Hophra, hearing of her beauty and talent, sent for her to Memphis, and offered to buy her of Charaxus, but the latter had already long, though secretly, given Rhodopis her freedom, and loved her far too well to allow of a separation. She, too, loved the handsome Lesbian and refused to leave him despite the brilliant offers made to her on all sides. At length Charaxus made this wonderful woman his lawful wife, and continued to live with her and her little daughter Kleïs in Naukratis, until the Lesbian exiles were recalled to their native land by Pittakus. He then started homeward with his wife, but fell ill on the journey, and died soon after his arrival at Mitylene. Sappho, who had derided her brother for marrying one beneath him, soon became an enthusiastic admirer of the beautiful widow and rivaled Alcaeus in passionate songs to her praise."

We may mention also in closing this chapter the lyrics, published in a small volume, called *Stürme*, by Carmen Sylva, the nom de plume of Rumania's late queen, because in these lyrics the tragedy of Sapphic love has a German political rather than a Lesbian setting.

X. SAPPHO IN FRENCH LITERATURE [168]

THE POETESS of passion, perfect in expression, is more akin to French literature than to German, and so it is not surprising to discover Sapphic echoes in every period of the former from that of the erudite and artistic poetry of the Pléiade in the sixteenth century to the present day of Maurice Donnay. In the sixteenth century Louise Labé was composing sonnets which burned like an ode of Sappho, and in 1556 Remy Belleau in his *Anacréon* published the first French translation of Sappho. Only three years later (1559), another of the Pléiade, Pierre de Ronsard, who turned from his admiration of Homer and Pindar to Horace, Anacreon, and Sappho, gave in the second book of his *Amours*, a translation of the second ode of Sappho:

Je suis un demy-dieu quand, assis vis-à-vis
De toy, mon cher souci, j'escoute des devis,
Devis entre-rompus d'un gracieux sourire,
Souris qui me retient le coeur emprisonné:

Car, en voyant tes yeux, je me pasme étonné
Et de mes pauvres flancs un seul vent je ne tire.
Ma langue s'engourdit, un petit feu me court
Fretillant sous la peau; je suis muet et sourd
Et une obscure nuit dessus mes yeux demeure;
Mon sang devient glacé, l'esprit fuit de mon corps,
Je tremble tout de crainte, et peu s'en faut alors
Qu'à tes pieds estendu sans âme je ne meure.

Ronsard also translated the famous folk-song, which has been so much imitated in all literatures, wrongly calling it an epigram: [169]

Desia la Lune est couchée,
La poussiniere est cachée,
Et ia la my-nuit brunette
Vers l'Aurore s'est panchée,
Et ie dors au lict seulette.

In the second book of his *Poèmes a Christophile de Choiseul* (Edition Laumonier V, 186), Ronsard (1556) said:

Le doux Anacreon me plaist et ie voudrois que la
  douce Saphon
Qui si bien resueilloit la lyre Lesbienne,
En France accompaignast la Muse Teïenne!

Early in the seventeenth century Malherbe wrote the following stanzas for le Duc de Bellegarde "to a lady who imagined that he was in love with her," in which he copied from the Lesbian poetess certain symptoms of love:

> Philis, qui me voit le teint blême,
> Les sens ravis hors de moi-même,
> Et les yeux trempés tout le jour,
> Cherchant la cause de ma peine,
> Se figure, tant elle est vaine,
> Qu'elle m'a donné de l'amour . . .
> En quelle école nonpareille
> Auroit-elle appris la merveille
> De si bien charmer ses appas,
> Que je pusse la trouver belle,
> Pâlir, transir, languir pour elle
> Et ne m'en apercevoir pas?

In 1620 Colletet published a prose imitation of Ovid, entitled *Lettre de Saphon à Phaon* (*Les Epistres d'Ovide. Traduites en prose françoise. Par les sieurs Du Perron, Des Portes, de la Brosse, de Lingendes, Hedelin et Colletet. Paris, 1620*). In 1660 Le Sieur Du Four translated the two odes, the first in prose, the second in verse. In 1674 that great classicist, Nicholas Boileau, who ranked the ancient writers above the modern because they had been tested through hundreds of years and because they agreed with nature and reason, included a

beautiful and truly classical rendering of the
second ode, in his translation of the *Treatise on
the Sublime:*

*Je sens de veine en veine une subtile flamme
Courir par tout mon corps sitôt que je te vois;
Et dans les doux transports où s'égare mon âme
Je ne saurais trouver de langue ni de voix.
Un nuage confus se répand sur ma vue;
Je n'entends plus, je tombe en de douces langueurs;
Et pâle, sans haleine, interdite, éperdue,
Un frisson me saisit, je tremble, je me meurs.*

In 1677 Boileau's intimate friend, Jean Racine,
produced his great tragedy in five acts, *Phèdre*,
based mainly on Euripides and Seneca, but
including a translation of Sappho's second ode,
in Act I, scene 3, where Phaedra says about
Hippolytus:

*Je le vis, je rougis, je pâlis à sa vue;
Un trouble s'éleva dans mon âme éperdue;
Mes yeux ne voyoient plus, je ne pouvois parler;
Je sentis tout mon corps et transir et brûler;
Je reconnus Vénus et ses feux redoutables,
D'un sang qu'elle poursuit tourments inévitables.*

Racine's comment was that he had "rien vu de
plus vif ni de plus beau dans toute l'antiquité."
In 1649 Mlle de Scudéry in her *Artamène ou le*

[163]

Grand Cyrus and also in her letters calls herself
Sappho, perhaps thinking of Sappho as a great
literary writer and with a reference to Platonic
friendship but no conception of Sappho as a bad
character. Bayle rather objects to giving the
name Sappho to a "fille qui écrivoit parfaitement
bien en vers et en prose, et dont la vertu étoit
admirée." Perhaps Anne Dacier was not then
the first to defend Sappho. In any case, Mlle de
Scudéry gives the wrong idea of the historical
Sappho, for in the tenth volume of *le Grand
Cyrus* she gives a tedious recital of the loves of
Sappho and Phaon. What could be farther
from the real burning Sappho than desiring
"un amant sans vouloir un mari, mais un amant
qui, se contentant de la possession de son coeur,
l'aime avec respect jusqu'à la mort." The later
French romance, entitled *Les Amours de Sapho
et de Phaon*, also has nothing to do with the real
Sappho. In 1680 Hilaire-Bernard de Requeleyne
(cf. Baillet, *Jugemens des Savans*, IV. 392–393)
gave with the Greek a poetical version, and
in the next year Professor Le Fèvre of the
University of Saumur, the Greek scholar and
translator of Virgil, made another French
translation, which was disloyal to the Greek
and did not deserve the praise which has

been bestowed upon it. On December 1, 1681,[170] his daughter, Anne (Madame Dacier) published *Les Poësies d'Anacreon et de Sapho* with notes and a life of Sappho. She believed in the Phaon story and that Sappho followed Phaon to Sicily and there composed the "plus beaux vers du monde," including the hymn to Venus; "Tout le monde sçait qu'elle aima Phaon et qu'elle l'aima d'une manière fort violente."

"Ce qui me fait croire qu'il ne faut pas ajoûter foy à tout ce que l'on trouve écrit contre elle. Si elle avoit esté de l'humeur dont on l'a dépeinte, il n'y a point d'apparence qu'elle eût eu tant de chagrin de l'amour de Caraxus, ni qu'elle eût osé l'en reprendre avec tant d'éclat. Il ne faut pas douter que son merite ne luy eût fait bien des ennemis; car elle surpassoit en sçavoir, non seulement toutes les femmes, quoi que de son temps il y en eût en Grece d'extrémement sçavantes; mais elle estoit même fort au dessus des plus excellens Poëtes. Je crois donc que ceux dont les vers auroient esté trouvez incomparables, si Sapho n'en eût jamais fait, ne furent pas de ses amis, et que l'envie a fait écrire les calomnies dont on a tâché de la noircir. Je ne puis même m'imaginer que les Mityleniens eussent eu tant de veneration pour une personne si décriée, et qu'aprés sa mort, ils eussent fait graver son image sur leur monoye."

Sappho's name was in vogue at this time wherever love was the subject of conversation

or of writing. In 1683 Bernard le Bovier de
Fontenelle in his *Dialogues des morts*,[171] a title
taken from Lucian, has *Sapho* and *Laure* discuss which sex should be the aggressor in love-
making. Fontenelle displays no knowledge of
Sappho herself, but has chosen her name, like
so many writers even down to the time of
Alphonse Daudet, to lend importance to a story
which has already been conceived and for which
an attractive title must be found. We can only
quote the latter part of the dialogue:

LAURE. Quoi! auriez-vous voulu qu'on eût établi
que les femmes attaqueraient les hommes?

SAPHO. Eh! quel besoin y a-t-il que les uns
attaquent, et que les autres se défendent? Qu'on
s'aime de part et d'autre autant que le cœur en dira.

LAURE. Oh! les choses iraient trop vite, et
l'amour est un commerce si agréable, qu'on a bien
fait de lui donner le plus de durée que l'on a pu.
Que serait-ce, si l'on était reçu des que l'on s'offri-
rait? Que deviendraient tous ces soins qu'on prend
pour plaire, toutes ces inquiétudes que l'on sent,
quand on se reproche de n'avoir pas assez plu, tous
ces empressemens avec lesquels on cherche un
moment heureux, enfin tout cet agréable mélange
de plaisirs et de peine qu'on appelle amour? Rien
ne serait plus insipide, si l'on ne faisait que s'entr'-
aimer.

SAPHO. Hé bien, s'il faut que l'amour soit une
espèce de combat, j'aimerais mieux qu'on eût obligé
les hommes à se tenir sur la défensive. Aussi-bien,

ne m'avez-vous pas dit que les femmes avaient plus de penchant qu'eux à la tendresse? A ce compte, elles attaqueraient mieux.

LAURE. Oui, mais ils se défendraient trop bien. Quand on veut qu'un sexe résiste, on veut qu'il résiste autant qu'il faut pour faire mieux goûter la victoire à celui qui attaque, mais non pas assez pour la remporter. Il doit n'être ni si faible, qu'il se rende d'abord, ni si fort, qu'il ne se rende jamais. C'est là notre caractère, et ce ne serait peut-être pas celui des hommes. Croyez-moi, après qu'on a bien raisonné ou sur l'amour, ou sur telle autre matière qu'on voudra, on trouve au bout du compte que les choses sont bien comme elles sont, et que la réforme qu'on prétendrait y apporter gâterait tout.

In 1684 une Demoiselle de qualité de la Province de Guienne, only eighteen years of age, published a French prose translation of the two odes in the *Mercure* for July. In the same year appeared a metrical translation with Greek text, philological notes, and a life of Sappho in which are repeated the stories of disgraceful love, infatuation for Phaon, and the Leucadian Leap, *Les Poésies d'Anacreon et de Sapho traduites de Grec en vers François*. In 1692 we have another verse rendering by Baron de Longuepierre, who added a feeble poem in which Apollo vainly defends Sappho against the arrows of love. In 1694 Despréaux in his edition of the *Treatise on*

the Sublime gave a poetical version of the second
ode which was so artistic that French critics
in their enthusiasm pronounced it superior to
the original, but its rhetorical phrases are far
from the simplicity of Sappho's Greek. Toward
the end of the grand siècle La Fare, the Epi-
curean and inseparable friend of the Abbé de
Chaulieu, translated the famous second ode.
In 1704 appeared a verse translation by De la
Fosse; in 1712 Gacon's verse translation of
Sappho's two odes and Father Bougeant's *Anacréon à Sapho, Dialogue en Vers Grecs;* and in
1713 appeared in French verse an imaginary
epistle of Sappho to Phaon (*Mercure* for April).
In 1716 La Fosse published his verses based on
those of the Le Fèvres. In 1758 Poinsinet de
Sivry produced his good verse translations.
Voltaire (1694–1778) made an elegant adapta-
tion of the second ode, with his eye also on
Theocritus' second idyl:

> *Reine des nuits, dis quel fut mon amour,*
> *Comme en mon sein les frissons et la flamme*
> *Se succédaient, me perdaient tour à tour;*
> *Quels doux transports égarèrent mon âme;*
> *Comment mes yeux cherchaient en vain le jour.*
> *Comme j'aimais et sans songer à plaire,*
> *Je ne pouvais ni parler ni me taire.*

In 1766 appeared Blin de Sainmore's *Lettres de Sapho a Phaon* with an account of Sappho's life and verse translations of her poems. In 1773 appeared a new version of Sappho in prose by Moutonnet de Clairfons which proved so popular that it went through at least seven editions. In 1798 Mérard de Saint-Just published his verse translations of Sappho and Anacreon. Toward the end of the eighteenth century,[172] an imaginary Greek manuscript, said to have been found at Herculaneum, translated by de Lantier, was published under the title *Voyages d'Antenor en Grèce et en Asie*, a most interesting and learned story of an imaginary trip to Grecian lands. Antenor and Phanor in the first chapter of the second volume meet Sappho and two unfortunate Greeks. An account is given in chapter three of the love of Sappho and Phaon, and the hymn to Aphrodite, quoted in the notes in Boileau's translation, is addressed to Phaon: "C'est pour cet ingrat qu'un jour dans l'enthousiasme de la poésie et de l'amour, je composai cette ode qui a circulé dans toute la Grèce, et que sans doute la postérité répétera encore." In the fourth chapter Antenor and his friend attend the funeral of Sappho and see the ashes

deposited in an urn. On the cippus is carved
a lyre with this epitaph:

> Ci-gît Sapho, la gloire de nos jours;
> Muses, pleurez, pleurez, Amours.

In the seventh chapter an account is given of
Sappho's last days, and Theagenes is revealed
as her rival, to whom Phaon has united himself
by a solemn bond. To Sappho is attributed a
long ode in which she invokes Venus and all the
infernal deities against her lover. She ends,
however, by returning to the sweetness and
generosity which had originally characterized
her. I quote only the last two stanzas:

> Et toi, mes amours, ô ma lyre,
> Douce compagne de mes jeux,
> Repose toi, ma muse expire;
> Reçois ici mes longs adieux.
>
> Mourons; allons au noir rivage:
> Heureuse, si, dans mon ennui,
> De Phaon emportant l'image,
> Je peux aux morts parler de lui.

The author evidently was fond of Sappho and
would compare with her Louise Labbé, la belle
Cordière (1526–1566), a woman of tender heart
and with a taste for passion, who wrote verses

on love in Greek, Latin, Italian, French, and Spanish. At this time Sappho was held in high esteem and it was a compliment to call a writer "a modern Sappho." So for example in the preface to L'Abbé Le Roy, *Le Paradis perdu*, poëme traduit de l'Anglais de Milton en vers françois (Rouen, 1775) we read: "Aussi a-t-on fait le plus favorable et le plus juste accueil à la charmante esquisse du Paradis Terrestre, que daigna nous donner une femme célébre, dont le nom seul fait l'éloge, Mme du Boccage, cette Sappho moderne, qui fait d'honneur a la France."

In 1777 [173] Sauvigny published his *Poésies de Sapho*, composed of eighteen odes, four *scolies morales*, four epigrams, the epitaphs of Timas and Pelagon, some fragments, a letter of Sappho to Phaon, and a hymn to Venus. There are many pretty uses of Sappho, though in no sense can the poems be said to be those of Sappho. The third ode is an echo of the fragment on the Evening Star:

Belle étoile du soir, digne ornement des cieux,

. . . .

Tu fais rentrer le paisible troupeau,
Qui du loup ravisseur craint la dent meurtrière;
La fille qui, joyeuse, a quitté le hameau,
Tu la ramènes à sa mère.

[171]

Ces timides amans que Vénus a touchés,
  Qui brûlent d'être unis ensemble,
Et que l'éclat du jour avait tenus cachés,
  C'est ton retour qui les rassemble.

The fifth ode renders the fragment on virginity:

  La Jeune Épousée.
Rose de la pudeur que l'amour a cueillie,
Votre premier éclat me sera-t-il rendu?

  La Virginité.
Ingrate, vous l'avez perdu;
Vous l'avez perdu pour la vie.

The sixth ode is simply Boileau's translation of
the Aphrodite hymn. The thirteenth, addressed
to Atthis, combines two fragments:

La lune au front d'argent et sa cour lumineuse
    Echappent à mes yeux;
D'un voile plus obscur la nuit silencieuse
    Enveloppe les cieux.

Heure que j'attendais, qui dut m'être si chère,
Tu t'es évanouie, et je suis seule, ô dieux!

The fifteenth ode is a dialogue between Alcaeus
and Sappho, and the note interprets as Sappho's
refusal of Alcaeus the famous fragment of which
a Latin version is given:

Si nobis amicus es, torum accipe junior;
Non enim sustinebo convescere cum seniore,
Dum junior sim.

Other writers of the end of the eighteenth century who paid tribute to Sappho were Bernis in his ode *Harmonie*, Lebrun in his epigrams, Parny in his *Journée champêtre*, La Harpe, who knew only ode II, and M. Legouvé who writes:

Vois Sapho; par Phaon trahie
Elle rendit son art confident de ses pleurs
Et merita la gloire en chantant ses malheurs.

Other French translators of about this time are Regnier Desmarais, Ricard, Langeac, Deguerle, Marchena, Blin de Sainmore, Abbé Batteux, and Gorsse in *Journal des Muses* III.

In the nineteenth century the echoes and translations of Sappho are even more numerous. The first of the neo-classicists, André Chénier, follower of Boileau, owed much of his enthusiasm for the Greeks to his Greek mother, and imitated Sappho in the ode which he wrote for his love, the ode so admired by Alfred de Musset, the charming poet who also knew the sufferings of love:

Fanny, l'heureux mortel qui près de toi respire
Sait, à te voir parler, et rougir, et sourire
De quels hôtes divins le ciel est habité . . .

He also used the fragment about Virginity (Latouche edition I, p. 64). Jacques Delille, the famous translator of Virgil, and the great representative of didactic and descriptive poetry, in his *Poésies fugitives* (1802) made a good literal translation. In the same year Vanderbourg published some verses camouflaged as the *Poésies* de Madame Clotilde de Surville, who was supposed to have lived 1405–1495. He gives a translation of the famous second ode, of which I quote only the last stanza:

S'ennuagent mes yeux: n'oy plus qu'ennuy, rumeurs,
Je brûle, je languis; chauds frissons dans ma veine
Circulent: je pâlis, je palpite, l'haleine
    Me manque, je me meurs.

The two great initiators of Romanticism also knew Sappho. Madame de Staël wrote (1811) a drama published 1821, *Sapho*, in which Phaon is divided between love for two different women. Chateaubriand in 1809 in *Les Martyrs* [174] makes Cymodocée, who was on the point of becoming a Christian and already betrothed to Eudore, a fervent disciple of Christ, say to her fiancé: "Dis-moi, puisqu'on peut aimer dans ton culte, il y a donc une Vénus chrétienne? . . . Le colère de cette déesse est-elle redoutable? Force-t-elle la jeune fille à chercher le jeune homme dans la palestre, à l'introduire furtivement sous le toit paternel? Ta Vénus rend-elle la langue embarrassée? Répand-elle un feu brûlant, un froid mortel dans les veines?" Chateaubriand adds here (and also in *Revolutions Anciennes*) Boileau's translation and in the same place he cites the passage from Racine's *Phèdre* which we have quoted, p.163. In 1805 L. Gorsse published *Sapho, poëme en dix chants*.[175] He defends Sappho's character (eleven years before the German Welcker) but believes that her love for Phaon was "un fait incontestable, dont tous les genres de littérature ont le droit, de s'emparer." He speaks of the Abbé Barthélemy, who in *Voyage d'Anacharsis* paints "les transports et l'ardeur de Sapho;" also of Lantier, *Voyages d'Anténor*, who had placed Sappho in such a bright light that he has brought out new beauties in the subject, which had not been seen previously. Both quote Boileau's translation. Gorsse also praises, as possessing a grace which men can never attain, the fragments of poetry which two ladies, Mesdames de Beaufort-d'Haut-poul and Caroline Wougne, published under the name of *Sapho*. On pages 181–187 (Vol.II) he quotes a romance by each, attributed to Sappho, which deals with her love for Phaon. In that of Caroline Wougne Sappho meets Phaon on his return from Sicily during a stormy night in a country house where he is asking for hospitality. Gorsse has also consulted Madame Pipelet de Salm, who presented Sappho on the lyric stage with grace and dignity. He himself unites the legends of her love with those of her writings, and drawing also on Tibullus, Propertius, Virgil, Lucretius, and especially Ovid, makes Sappho speak as poetess and lover fifty expanded elegies. There are five in each of the ten cantos besides a prologue and epilogue. In view of the fact that none of Sappho's elegies are extant, the reconstruction, though fanciful, is extremely interesting. The first five songs picture Sappho's desire, contentment, happiness, fear, and calmness. Phaon is jealous of Alcaeus and proposes to leave Lesbus to dwell in the Vale of Tempe, but Sappho asks Phaon to share in her poems, which will immortalize their love, and then reveals to him the origin of music. The second five represent her suspicion, grief, torment, and pursuit of Phaon to Sicily, her despair and the Leucadian Leap, after she sees Phaon making eyes at Telesilla. In the fifth elegy of

[176]

the first canto is an adaptation of Sappho's second ode, in which the first verse addressed to Phaon is taken without acknowledgment from André Chénier's *Fanny*. Phaon seems to be the principal figure, and the legends about him are tremendously expanded with the help of many Greek myths. As in so many other writers he becomes a great athlete and must overcome his opponents in the stadium. The Italian author of *Avventure di Saffo* had done likewise and made Phaon win with the same throw which Ulysses used in Homer. The *Voyages d'Anténor* had made Phaon first appear to Sappho after winning in the gymnasium. Likewise Gorsse has Sappho see Phaon for the first time in the stadium at Mytilene. There she describes the impression Phaon made on her, when he won the athletic prize. All these writers forget, however, that women in Sappho's day were not allowed to witness the nude athletic contests. Gorsse shows his wide acquaintance with the ancient accounts of Sappho when in the fourth elegy of the second canto he mentions: "un foible enfant, Cléis, qui t'est si chère!" With only a few errors he represents all the many friends and pupils of Sappho, — to whom he gives classical epithets, — as help-

ing Sappho to preserve Phaon's love. He is as
keen as the modern critics when he says in a
note that Erinna cannot be the famous poet,
but he is wrong in picturing *Brune Andromède*
and *Blonde Gorgo* as friends or pupils rather
than rivals of Sappho.

O vous, *pourtant, qui faites mes délices,*
Du noeud sacré qui vous attache à moi,
J'attends encor les plus tendres offices,
Je les réclame au nom de votre foi.

Blanche Cydno, délicate Amynthone,
Douce Pyrine, intéressante Athis,
Brune Andromède, agréable Gellone,
Blonde Gorgo, séduisante Mnaïs!

Par vos attraits, par vos grâces naïves,
Auprès de moi captivez mon amant;
Pour qu'il y trouve un doux enchantement,
Soyez sans cesse à lui plaire attentives.

Vous dont Euterpe anime les accens,
Belle Mégare, adorable Gyrinne,
Docte Gougile, ingénieuse Erinne,
Pour le charmer adressez-lui vos chants.

Vous qui brillez dans l'art de Therpsycore,
Aimable Eunique, élégante Anagore,
Devant ses yeux, avec agilité,
Formez les pas qu'aime la volupté.

[178]

Toi, *Damophile, ornement de la Grèce,*
Dis *à Phaon qu'au milieu des neuf Soeurs*
J'ai *quelquefois, sur les bords du Permesse,*
Respiré *l'air qu'y parfument les fleurs.*

Et *toi, surtout, sensible Télésile,*
Accorde-moi *ton bienfaisant secours,*
Pour *conserver Phaon à mes amours,*
Que *ton esprit en moyens soit fertile.*

Dans *ses regards interroge ses goûts,*
De *ses desirs occupe-toi sans cesse,*
Pour *que mon coeur par tes soins les connoisse,*
Et *qu'aisément il les prévienne tous.*

Parmi *les sons dont retentit ma lyre,*
Répète-lui *ceux que Vénus m'inspire;*
Et, *par l'objet dont il est adoré,*
Qu'il *ait l'orgueil de se voir honoré.*

Toutes, *enfin, ô mes tendres amies!*
A *mon amant composez une cour;*
Le *doux lien dont nous sommes unies*
S'affermira *par les noeuds de l'amour.*

The second elegy in the fourth canto has a
pretty imitation of the famous third fragment.
Sappho dissuades Phaon from his jealousy of
Alcaeus, which of course is not an ancient
legend, in the following words:

[179]

Comme un léger brouillard fuit aux rayons du jour,
Que ton soupçon expire à la voix de l'amour!
Sois sans crainte, Phaon! Contre un sexagénaire
Est-ce à toi de lutter dans l'art heureux de plaire?
A toi dont la jeunesse et les riants attraits
Du chantre de Lesbos effacent les succès,
Autant qu'on voit Diane effacer la lumière
De ces astres dorés dont se pare la nuit,
Quand l'éclat argenté du char qu'elle conduit
Annonce que des cieux elle ouvre la barrière?

In the third elegy of the same canto is an elaboration of the fragment on the power of love, the bitter-sweet irresistible creature, and in the first elegy of the fifth canto there is an echo of the fragment about wealth without virtue. In long notes on the second elegy of the fifth book Gorsse cites de Sivry's or Sauvigny's verse translations or paraphrases in French, and Latin versions of a score of other fragments and of the Pelagon and Timas epitaphs. In the first elegy of the sixth canto the Sapphic symptoms of love are used:

Je sens mes cheveux se dresser,
Mon sang brûler d'une flamme rapide,
Ou dans mes veines se glacer.

The third elegy of the same canto is an adaptation of the hymn to Aphrodite and in the notes

[180]

are given Latin versions by Gorsse himself, Elias Andreas, and Birkow.

Not many have written elegies on Sappho, but Gorsse was followed in 1812 by Touzet, who wrote *Sapho, poëme élégiaque*. It was in 1816 that Lamartine wrote his mediocre imitation of Sappho's great hymn, calling it *L'élégie antique*. It is in the cold restored pseudo-classical style of Casimir Delavigne:

Dieux, quels transports nouveaux! ô dieux, comment décrire
Tous les feux dont mon sein se remplit à la fois?
Ma langue se glaça, je demeurai sans voix,
Et ma tremblante main laissa tomber ma lyre.

Here is Lamartine's own comment: "Un soir, en rentrant d'une de ces excursions, pendant laquelle nous avions relu la strophe unique, mais brûlante, de Sapho, sorte de Vénus de Milo, pareille à ce débris découvert par M. de Marcellus, qui contient plus de beauté dans un fragment qu'il n'y en a dans tout un musée de statues intactes, je m'enfermai, et j'écrivis le commencement grec de cette élégie ou de cette *héroïde . . .*" In one of his *Nouvelles Méditations poétiques* (not printed till 1823) he describes the suffering of the abandoned Sappho and her last, farewell words to the world and to life, before her suicide; the last line is: "adieu chère Lesbos à Vénus consacrée." Lamartine was followed in his idea of Sappho by Verlaine (1844–1896), the prince of the French poets after the death of Leconte de Lisle. Verlaine speaks of Sappho as "furieuse, les yeux caves et les seins roides." In writing to his friend Virieu, April 8, 1819, Lamartine mentions the fact that he has planned an opera on Jephté and adds that he is thinking of writing one on Sappho, which, however, was never written: "J'en ai un qui me brûle, c'est une Sapho, superbe sujet d'un opéra pareil."

In 1815 came *Sapho*, poème en trois chants par C. T. In 1820 Lazare Carnot published an excellent verse translation of the second ode, *Les Symptomes d'Amour*, and in 1827 E. Veïssier-Descombes, a translator also of Anacreon, published his classic rendering. In 1828 followed the poetical version of Cousin and Girodet; in 1835, Breghot du Lut., in prose and poetry; in 1836 Alexandre Hope's *Sapho*, a poem of about ten pages; in 1843, prose renderings in Michaud's *Biographie Universelle;* in 1847, Marullot et Grosset, in verse. In 1842, in the *Cariatides*, Théodore de Banville, one of the last

of the Romantic poets, that Greek "clown" of
France, wrote these verses on Sappho:

> ET TOI, *grande Sappho, reine de Mitylène!*
> *Lionne que l'Amour furieux enchaîna.*
> *Près de la mer grondante, avec son Erinna,*
> *Elle enseignait le rhythme et ses délicatesses*
> *Au troupeau triomphal des jeunes poétesses,*
> *Et glacée et brûlante, au bruit amer des flots*
> *Elle mêlait ses cris de rage et ses sanglots.*
> *O toi qui nous atteins avec des flèches sûres,*
> *De quels feux tu brûlas et de quelles blessures*
> *Son chaste sein meurtri par le baiser du vent!*
> *Mais comme rien ne meurt de ce qui fut vivant,*
> *Sa colère amoureuse et de souffrance avide,*
> *Plus tard devait dicter sa plainte au fier Ovide,*
> *Qui, choisissant l'amour, eut la meilleure part,*
> *Et frémir dans les vers d'Horace et de Ronsard.*

Baudelaire (1821–1867), the morbid realist,
uses the story of the Leucadian Leap in his
Lesbos:

> — *L'oeil d'azur est vaincu par l'oeil noir que tachète*
> *Le cercle ténébreux tracé par les douleurs*
> *De la mâle Sapho, l'amante et le poète!*
> *Plus belle que Vénus se dressant sur le monde.*

In a literary fragment (1845), entitled *Sapho,*
he refers to a famous and remarkable tragedy

on Sappho which was to be published soon afterwards by Arsène Houssaye. He quotes some verses which are reminiscent of Sappho's second ode:

Oui, Phaon, je vous aime; et, lorsque je vous vois,
Je perds le sentiment et la force et la voix.
Je souffre tout le jour le mal de votre absence,
Mal qui n'égale pas l'heur de votre présence;
Si bien que vous trouvant, quand vous venez le soir,
La cause de ma joie et de mon désespoir,
Mon âme les compense, et sous les lauriers roses
Etouffe l'ellébore et les soucis moroses.

In 1873 we have a translation by Etienne Prosper Dubois-Gucham, *La Grecque Pléiade;* in 1878 that of P. L. Courier; in 1882, the verses of de la Roche. About this time J. Richepin published in his undated romance, *Grandes Amoureuses*, prose translations of several fragments, and in 1889 Paul Lenois made a prose version. In 1884, Alphonse Daudet, after writing a novel on French life and customs as a warning to young men, and picturing a courtesan carried upstairs in the arms of her lover, gave the courtesan and the novel the title of *Sapho*. Soon afterwards appeared anonymously Madame E. Caro's

[184]

Sapho. In 1895 were heard the songs of Pierre Louys, who in *Les chansons de Bilitis traduites du Grec pour la première fois* [176] transforms Mytilene into a modern Sodom and Sappho into the mistress of a band of *hetaerae*. He pretends that he is translating Greek poems that were found in excavating the poetess' grave on Amathus. He even represents them as published by a Doctor Heim of Leipzig. Further to mystify the reader Louys tells of some of the poems that have not been translated and marks restorations in the text, as if these songs had actually been found marred and mutilated and as if the archaeologist had restored the missing words. He even uses, to give a Greek atmosphere, many Greek expressions such as *Kypris Philommeïdès*. Many of his Greek forms, such as Dzeus, are absurd. Charming as are these *Bucoliques en Pamphylie*, *Élégies à Mitylène*, *Épigrammes dans l'île de Chypre*, they belong rather to' pornographic literature, as does his romance called *Aphrodite*, in which the pseudo-Lesbian idea of two girls marrying one another is to be found. Such bits of perverted Sapphism as appear in many other French writers have no place in the literature of the real Sappho, who can now, after the discovery of all the new papyri, easily be distinguished from the Sappho of romance and legend. Unfortunately the last French translation by Meunier (1911) does not include these recent relics.

One of the latest French imitations of Sappho is by that great reviver of Aristophanes, Maurice Donnay, whose comedies have attracted such large audiences in Europe. In his *Lysistrata* (Act I, scene II), Donnay makes the pretty Hirondelle as she walks along the shore of the violet sea recite to the accompaniment of the music of the waves the song which divine Sappho composed for the Egyptian courtesan Rhodopis, although we have no evidence for such a song:

> RHODOPIS, *ton amant est comme*
> U*n dieu: son bonheur me courrouce.*
> Q*uand je pense que c'est un homme*
> P*our qui ta voix se fait si douce,*
> E*t que c'est Charaxos, mon frère,*
> Q*ui possède ta chair superbe,*
> E*t ta Beauté dont j'étais fière,*
> J*e deviens plus verte que l'herbe.*
> M*es yeux se troublent, mes oreilles*
> S*'emplissent de murmures vagues*
> E*t de grandes rumeurs pareilles*
> A*u bruit que fait le choc des vagues.*

Et voilà qu'une sueur froide
Inonde tout mon corps qui tremble,
Puis, je reste sans souffle, et froide
Ainsi qu'un cadavre, il me semble
Que je meurs! que je meurs!

This, of course, is an echo of the famous second ode of Sappho which has influenced all ages and countries and continues so to do. Hardly a year passes without some translation or reminiscence of it in Greece or Italy, in France or Germany, in England or America.

XI. SAPPHO IN ENGLISH AND AMERICAN LITERATURE

SAPPHO was little read in England and as a writer of poetry probably did not exist, except for a few Englishmen of great learning, before the sixteenth century. Even in the seventeenth century Thomas Stanley, a man of considerable culture, omitted Sappho from his translation of Anacreon (1650). In the sixteenth and seventeenth centuries the imitations limit themselves to the Sapphic metre,[177] with the exception of the famous line in Ben Jonson's pastoral drama, *The Sad Shepherd* (Act II, 2): "But best the dear good angel of the spring, The nightingale," and of Sir Philip Sidney, who seems to have been entirely forgotten by modern writers on Sappho. But it is interesting to note, in the movement led by Gabriel Harvey in pre-Shakesperian days to write English poetry in classical metres, that sapphics were attempted by Harvey's friend, Sir Philip Sidney, in *The Countesse of Pembroke's Arcadia*, which was begun in 1580. One stanza will suffice to show

how strained were the strophes thus manu-
factured:

If *mine eyes can speak to do hearty errand,*
Or *mine eyes' language she do hap to judge of,*
So *that eyes' message be of her received,*
Ho*pe we do live yet.*

It is rather strange that Sir Philip did not use
this metre in his translation of the second ode
of Sappho, but employed anacreontics.

My *Muse, what ailes this ardor?*
Mine *eyes be dim, my limbs shake,*
My *voice is hoarse, my throat scorch'd,*
My *tongue to this my roof cleaves,*
My *fancy amaz'd, my thoughts dull'd,*
My *heart doth ake, my life faints,*
My *soul begins to take leave.*

This being a wholly iambic measure does not
appear so exotic as the sapphics. Indeed, the
youthful experimenter achieved a noteworthy
success in rhythmic effect by ending each line
with a foot composed of one strong syllable.

Most of the knowledge there was of Sappho
in the Elizabethan and Jacobean times, however, seems to have been superficially based
mainly on the Ovidian legend. Such a wonder-

ful story told by such a wonderful story-teller
interested the early classicists in England, and
the Phaon myth permeated much literature.
Ben Jonson (*Under-Woods*, No. 45) says:

> *Did Sappho, on her seven-tongu'd lute,*
> *So speak (as yet it is not mute)*
> *Of Phaon's form?*

Thomas Nashe in his novel, *The Unfortunate
Traveller* (1594), is a typical example: "Golde
easily bends, the most ingenious minds are
easiest moved, *Ingenium nobis molle Thalia
dedit*, said *Psapho* to *Phao*." It is just possible
that Robert Herrick (1591–1674), who published
so many poems to or upon *Sapho*, the name of
his own love, knew from Athenaeus the fragment (E. 62) "much whiter than an egg,"
when he published in *Hesperides*, No. 350
(1648) the verses:

> *Fain would I kiss my Julia's dainty leg,*
> *Which is as white and hair-less as an egge.*

John Lyly made Sappho an allegorical image
of the Virgin Queen: "I will ever be virgin,"
says Sappho. The play, *Sapho and Phao*, was
produced in 1584 in the presence of Queen
Elizabeth. Lyly makes Sappho a princess of

Syracuse and takes many liberties with the historical Sappho. Lyly's Sappho resembles the Queen, and Phao is supposed to be the Duke of Leicester, but in such an allegory all reference to the Leucadian Leap has to be omitted, and there are no echoes of Sappho's own fragments. When Phaon comes, Sappho soliloquizes: "Wilt thou open thy love? Yea? No, Sapho, but staring in his face till thine eyes dazzle and thy spirits faint, die before his face; then this shall be written on thy tomb, that though thy love were greater than wisdom could endure, yet thine honour was such as love could not violate." Aphrodite interrupts their love and Phaon says: "This shall be my resolution, wherever I wander, to be as I were kneeling before Sapho; my loyalty unspotted, though unrewarded . . . My life shall be spent in sighing and wishing, the one for my bad fortune, the other for Sapho's good." Even Robert Burton in that famous storehouse of quotations, his *Anatomy of Melancholy* (1621), does not know Sappho as a poetess, and refers only to the *Leucata Petra:* "Here leaped down that Lesbian Sappho for Phaon on whom she miserably doted, hoping thus to ease herself and to be freed of her love pangs." The first English translation

of Sappho's second ode (1652), quoted by Edwin
Cox, is John Hall's version in his translation
of the *Treatise on the Sublime*. He does not
mention Sidney, and Addison did not know even
Hall's translation or that of Pulteney, for he
says that the versions by Ambrose Philips in
1711 were the first. [In 1675 Edward Phillips
in his *Theatrum Poetarum* devoted a chapter to
Ancient Poetesses and Sappho.] He knew the
tradition of a second Sappho, but quoted no
fragments. In 1680 Pulteney, who had a knowledge of small Latin and less Greek, gave a
filtered translation from the French of the
Treatise on the Sublime and the second Sapphic
ode. In 1695 appeared another translation by
an unknown author, but it was not till 1711 that
any detailed study of Sappho began. In that
year, in the Spectator (nos. 223, 229, and 233),
Joseph Addison discussed Sappho at length.
Even then we have only the namby-pamby
verses of Ambrose Philips, so overpraised by
Addison. Soon followed translations by Herbert
in 1713, in his edition of Petronius (pp. 325–328);
and in 1719, by Green. In 1735 John Addison
published the works of Anacreon with Sappho
added, in which the *Loeb Classical Library* idea
of putting the Greek text on one page and the

translation on the opposite page was antici-
pated. Philips' version of the Aphrodite hymn
was forty-two lines long, but Addison gives one
of his own in twenty-eight lines, which is the
number in the original Greek. His own rendering is as good as that of Philips, which perhaps
is damning it with faint praise. His translations of the eight fragments which he includes
are also not remarkable. In 1748, we have
Tobias Smollett's version of the second ode in
Roderick Random. About 1745, Mark Akenside
in his tenth Ode on *Lyric Poetry* based a stanza
on Sappho's first ode. In 1760, "a Gentleman of Cambridge" published his verse translations. In some publications he is considered
to be different from Francis Fawkes, who undoubtedly is the gentleman referred to. In
1768 appeared E. B. Greene's free and mediocre
translation, in which Aphrodite's doves become
"feathered steeds," and which ignores the Sapphic metre. In 1796, Mrs. Mary Robinson published *Sappho and Phaon*, but these sonnets of
hers are not, as she claims, legitimate descendants
of the real Sappho.

It was not till the nineteenth century, however, that the actual literary remains of Sappho
were scientifically studied. In 1814, we have the

translations of Elton, in 1815 of Egerton, in 1833 the Sapphics by Merivale, in 1854 Palgrave, in 1877 Walhouse. In 1869, Edwin Arnold's *Poets of Greece* gave one of the best renderings of the Aphrodite hymn in Sapphic metre and included pretty translations of nine of her fragments. Edwin Arnold called her: "that exquisite poetess . . . whose genius among all feminine votaries of singing stands incontestably highest." He protests against Swinburne's repetition of the scandal against her sweet name which gossiping generations have invented; he rejects the Leucadian Leap and the Phaon myth. In 1871 T. W. Higginson wrote his important article on Sappho for *The Atlantic Monthly*, which can now be found in his *Atlantic Essays*. He translated several of the fragments and the hymn than which, he says, "there is not a lyrical poem in Greek literature nor in any other which has by its artistic structure inspired more enthusiasm." He subjects to many a hard blow that paltry Scot soul, Colonel Mure, whose history of Greek literature ought to be tabooed. He repudiates the calumnies of the comedians and scandal-mongers. His appreciation of Sappho is one of the best that has been written.

In 1883 J. A. Symonds published his translations, and some of them were made for and included in that charming little book of Wharton's, which appeared in its first edition in 1885. Even before Wharton, Swinburne had given his high estimate of Sappho and had melted together many of the fragments into his *Anactoria*. In 1894, Maurice Thompson published in *The Atlantic Monthly*, "The Sapphic Secret," and gave a fine appreciation of Sappho with translations of the shorter fragments. During the last thirty years the discovery of new papyri has stimulated interest in Sappho and many books and articles, scientific and popular, have been printed. For a discussion of the recovery of Greek literature from papyri and the difficulties involved in deciphering and restoring Sappho's new fragments, I refer the reader to my introduction on the subject in Miller-Robinson, *The Songs of Sappho*. I refer the reader to the bibliography for some of the books and to a note [178] for references to some popular articles, and call special attention to the volumes of Easby-Smith, Miss Patrick, Petersen, Edmonds, Cox, Tucker, and Edward Storer, most of whom give their own verse renderings of some, if not all, of Sappho's fragments. Many mod-

ern poets, both British and American, have
adapted or expanded Sappho's fragments in
English verse, Lucy Milburn, Bliss Carman,
Percy Osborn, that pure Pelasgian, John Myers
O'Hara. Recently Dr. Marion Mills Miller,
formerly of Princeton University, has published
metrical adaptations of all the old and new
fragments, which are graceful and witty. He
has also given the romance of Sappho's life in
verse and has made a new poetical translation
of Ovid's *Sappho to Phaon*. In the same volume
(cf. Bibliography), I have published the Greek
text of all Sappho with a literal translation and
two introductions. One deals with the recovery
and restoration of Sappho's relics and shows
the romance as well as the difficulties involved
in deciphering and restoring her poems. The
other discusses Sappho's life and works.

The influence of Sappho on English and
American literature has been large. We have
already shown this in our citations, as it seemed
better to quote some of the great English writers
when we were speaking of Sappho herself. Addison was devoted to her, but his contemporary,
Pope, by translating Ovid's *Sappho to Phaon*,
aggravated the ill-fame which Ovid had given
her. Pope often mentions her, but without

knowledge of the true Sappho. In *Moral Essays* (*Epistle* III, 121) we have the line: "Why she (Phryne) and Sappho raise that monstrous sum?", referring to Lady Montague and to Miss Skerrett, the latter of whom was the mistress and later the second wife of Sir Robert Walpole. Lady Mary (Montague) is alluded to also in *Epistle* II, 24:

> As *Sappho's diamonds with her dirty smock;*
> Or *Sappho at her toilet's greasy task,*
> With *Sappho fragrant at an evening mask.*

Also in the *Prologue to the Satires*, in the *Epistle to Dr. Arbuthnot*, 369, we read: "Sappho can tell you how this man was bit." Sappho is mentioned again in *Imitations of Horace* (*Satire* I, l. 83) and in *Satires of Dr. John Donne* (II, 6), in these words: "As who knows Sappho, smiles at other whores." In his letters to Cromwell, Pope often mentions two Sapphos, one his own and the other Cromwell's: "My service, pray, to the other Sappho, who it is to be hoped, has not yet cast herself headlong from any of the Leucades about London, although her Phaon lately fled from her into Lincolnshire." Even in the letter to Steele, when he makes acknowledgment to the "fine fragment of Sappho,"

Pope is disingenuous and affected, as he suppresses the name of Flatman, to whom he was really indebted.

Wordsworth, influenced probably by Welcker's defense, had a good opinion of Sappho (cf. the quotation, p. 247). But his dear friend, Sir Walter Scott, seems to be ignorant of her, though the lines on the *Evening Star*, which we have quoted (p. 64), sound strikingly Sapphic. Coleridge seems to echo the famous fragment about the pippin on the topmost bough in his *One Red Leaf on the Topmost Twig;* but as he shows no other influence of Sappho this is probably an accidental resemblance. Thomas Moore, as a translator of Anacreon with whom Sappho was generally linked, knew Sappho well and translated some of her fragments into Latin as well as English. His rendering of the *Weaving Song* is especially charming (cf. p. 79). Another contemporary Irish poet, the Reverend George Croly, tells how:

> *Passion gave the living breath*
> *That shook the chords of Sappho's lyre.*

Of the post-Revolution poets the bombastic Byron, who may have learned something about Sappho from his friend and editor, Thomas

[198]

Moore, refers to her most. In *Don Juan* (III, 107), he expands, none too well, into a stanza of eight the two lines in which Sappho has painted such a beautiful miniature landscape of re-united village life. As Livingstone says in *The Legacy of Greece* (p. 265): "the English genius is rich and lavish rather than restrained. It is less in its nature to write like Sappho." Was Livingstone not thinking also of Swinburne and many another modern poet who plays so many indistinct, un-Greek variations on that divine line: "I loved thee once, Atthis, in the long ago," which Mackail has called "just one sliding sigh and whisper of sound." There is an-other expansion by the poet laureate of Canada, which we have quoted in a note (p. 257). It is Byron who in *Don Juan* (III, 76) speaks of

> *The isles of Greece, the isles of Greece!*
> *Where burning Sappho loved and sung;*

and in *Don Juan* (II) he speaks of " Sappho, the sage bluestocking in whose grave   All those may leap who rather would be neuter." In the controversy between Byron and Boules with regard to the second ode, Byron says: "Is not this sublime and fierce love for one of her own sex? And is not Philips' translation of it in the mouths of all your women? And are the English schools or the English women the more corrupt for all this?" Byron echoes the element of fire which has so often been noted in Sappho's songs, by critics from Plutarch to Sara Teasdale. He knows the story derived from Ovid and Maximus of Tyre that she was dark (p. 35) and also the legend of the Lover's Leap (*Childe Harold*, II, 39–41):

> *Childe Harold sail'd, and pass'd the barren spot,*
> *Where sad Penelope o'erlook'd the wave;*
> *And onward view'd the mount, not yet forgot,*
> *The lover's refuge, and the Lesbian's grave.*
> *Dark Sappho! could not verse immortal save*
> *That breast imbued with such immortal fire?*

> *Childe Harold hail'd Leucadia's cape afar;*
>
> . . . .
>
> *But when he saw the evening star above*
> *Leucadia's far-projecting rock of woe,*
> *And hail'd the last resort of fruitless love,*
> *He felt, or deem'd he felt, no common glow.*

While Shelley and Keats do not have clear echoes of Sappho, they come nearer to her in spirit than any other modern poets; but, even so, Keats' sensuousness removes him from

Sappho. W. L. Courtney, in a very interesting article on *Sappho and Aspasia*,[178] says: "Shelley has the true lyrical note, and Keats some of that chiselled loveliness which makes each Sapphic stanza a masterpiece." One might even suspect that Shelley knew the second ode, at least in some secondary source, when he composed *To Constantia Singing*.

Women poets naturally have taken an interest in Sappho. Mrs. Hemans, the English lyrist (1793–1835), speaks of "Sappho's fervent heart." Elizabeth Barrett Browning seems to have known only the song of the rose to which we have referred above (p. 68). She is familiar with the Lover's Leap legend, as was Byron, for she speaks in *A Vision of Poets* of

> —*Sappho, with that gloriole*
> *Of ebon hair on calmèd brows*—
> *O poet-woman! none foregoes*
> *The leap, attaining the repose.*

In Matthew Arnold there is much classical influence, but *A Modern Sappho* has nothing of ancient Sappho. Walter Savage Landor,[179] who looked back to Greece from Rome and by his delightful dialogues made the ancient ages live again, is one of the few who decry Sappho. He seems to be jealous when he says that "Sappho is not the only poetess who has poured forth her melodies to Hesperus, or who had reason to thank him." He composes ten verses himself entitled *Sappho to Hesperus*, which are not like Sappho's at all. Likewise he takes eight lines to express the thought of the despair of the lovesick maiden over her faithless lover, which Sappho depicts in a better picture of a single couplet. Landor finds Sappho deficient in delicacy in her answer to Alcaeus and attributes to her an epigram about Alcaeus which she never wrote. He would obliterate no letter of the invocation to Hesperus by a tear of his. Among the poems of Sappho he finds one written in a different hand from the rest, which pleases him as much as any of them, but it reads like Landor and is inferior to what Sappho would have said. In *Simonidea* he tries his hand at the *Weaving Song*:

> *Mother I cannot mind my wheel*
> *My fingers ache, my lips are dry,*
> *Oh if you felt the pain I feel!*
> *But oh, who ever felt as I?*

Charles Kingsley wrote a beautiful poem on Sappho, which well represents her mood; but there is hardly even a faint echo of Sappho's own fragments unless the words "all her veins ran fever" are accidentally suggested by the second ode.

SAPPHO

She lay among the myrtles on the cliff;
Above her glared the noon; beneath, the sea,
Upon the white horizon Atho's peak
Weltered in burning haze; all airs were dead;
The cicale slept among the tamarisk's hair;
The birds sat dumb and drooping. Far below
The lazy sea-weed glistened in the sun;
The lazy sea-fowl dried their steaming wings;
The lazy swell crept whispering up the ledge,
And sank again. Great Pan was laid to rest;
And Mother Earth watched by him as he slept,
And hushed her myriad children for a while.
She lay among the myrtles on the cliff;
And sighed for sleep, for sleep that would not hear,
But left her tossing still; for night and day
A mighty hunger yearned within her heart,
Till all her veins ran fever; and her cheek,
Her long thin hands, and ivory-channelled feet,
Were wasted with the wasting of her soul.
Then peevishly she flung her on her face,
And hid her eyeballs from the blinding glare,
And fingered at the grass, and tried to cool
Her crisp hot lips against the crisp hot sward:

And then she raised her head, and upward cast
Wild looks from homeless eyes, whose liquid light
Gleamed out between deep folds of blue-black hair,
As gleam twin lakes between the purple peaks
Of deep Parnassus, at the mournful moon.
Beside her lay her lyre. She snatched the shell,
And waked wild music from its silver strings;
Then tossed it sadly by. — 'Ah, hush!' she cries,
'Dead offspring of the tortoise and the mine!
Why mock my discords with thine harmonies?
Although a thrice-Olympian lot be thine,
Only to echo back in every tone
The moods of nobler natures than thine own.'

(CHARLES KINGSLEY)

William Cory, famous translator of the
Heraclitus epigram, who published poems on
Stesichorus and other classical subjects, prettily
transformed one of the fragments into:

Woman dead, lie there;
No record of thee
Shall there ever be,
Since thou dost not share
Roses in Pieria grown.
In the deathful cave,
With the feeble troop
Of the folk that droop,

[204]

Lurk and flit and crave,
Woman severed and far-flown.

William Morris, a fine classical scholar, as shown in his *Life and Death of Jason*, in *The Earthly Paradise* (1868–1871), expands in a very readable form the story of the Egyptian courtesan, Rhodopis, whom Sappho's brother, Charaxus, ransomed. About the same time (1870) Rossetti made the combination of two fragments which we have mentioned above (p. 93). Some tell us that Oscar Wilde's heart goes out to Sappho, but so far as I have read I have not been able to find in him any trace of the real Sappho.[178a] On the other hand, Tennyson and Swinburne read her fragments over and over. Tennyson, who thought the Sapphics of Horace to be "much inferior to those of Sappho," beautifully paraphrases the second ode in *Eleänore* (1832). In the original edition of *Fatima* (Dec. 1832), published under the title *O Love, Love, Love*, he prefixed the first line of this ode as a motto. Many as are the echoes of the sweet-bitter, bitter-sweet antithesis of Sappho (E. 81, above, p. 57) in Wharton and other critics, it seems strange that perhaps the most beautiful and deep-hearted of all, Elaine's song in Tennyson's Idyl is never cited, so far as I know.[180]

Love, art thou sweet? then bitter death must be:
Love, thou art bitter; sweet is death to me.
O Love, if death be sweeter, let me die.

Tennyson echoes the third fragment, as we have seen (p. 63); and he re-echoes through Horace another fragment in his *Epilogue* (p. 36). In *Fatima*, "Love, O withering might" suggests another fragment. In *Leonine Elegiacs* we have a better adaptation than in Byron of the Hesperus hymn:

The ancient poetess singeth, that Hesperus all
*   things bringeth,*
Smoothing the wearied mind: bring me my
*   love, Rosalind.*

In *Locksley Hall Sixty Years After* he again uses the same Sapphic fragment: "Hesper, whom the poet call'd the Bringer home of all good things." His brother, Frederick Tennyson, who was such a good Greek scholar that he won the medal at Trinity College for a Greek poem, in his *Isles of Greece* (1890) used several adaptations and translations of Sappho, the prettiest being those about Sappho's child Cleïs, about Hesper and the summer noonday siesta by the cool waters. Many writers of lyrics in England and Scotland have thought of Sappho, but generally of the Phaon story, as recently did Thomas McKie in his *Lyric on Love:* [181]

> *Bewildered with her love and grief,*
> *From lone Leucadia's stormy steep*
> *Distracted Sappho sought relief,*
> *By plunging in the whelming deep.*
> *The deep that closed upon her woes*
> *Not half so wild, impetuous flows.*

Swinburne is one of Sappho's greatest admirers, and we have quoted some of his praises among the appreciations of Sappho (p. 11). We have cited Noyes' appreciation of Swinburne's love of Sappho, and here are Thomas Hardy's interesting lines to Swinburne:

> — His *singing-mistress verily was no other*
> *Than she the Lesbian, she the music-mother*
> *Of all the tribe that feel in melodies;*
> *Who leapt, love-anguished, from the Leucadian steep*
> *Into the rambling world-encircling deep*
>   *Which hides her where none sees.*

> *And one can hold in thought that nightly here*
> *His phantom may draw down to the water's brim,*
> *And hers come up to meet it, as a dim*
> *Lone shine upon the heaving hydrosphere,*
> *And mariners wonder as they traverse near,*
>   *Unknowing of her and him.*

One dreams him sighing to her spectral form:
"O teacher, where lies hid thy burning line;
Where are those songs, O poetess divine
Whose very arts are love incarnadine?"
And her smile back: "Disciple true and warm,
*   Sufficient now are thine." . . .*

(THOMAS HARDY, *A Singer Asleep*)

While perhaps Swinburne exaggerates in his praise of Sappho, he owes much to the great poetess of love:

Love's priestess, mad with pain and joy of song,
Song's priestess, mad with joy and pain of love.
(*On the Cliffs*)

He makes her say:

My blood was hot wan wine of love,
And my song's sound the sound thereof,
The sound of the delight of it.

In *Tristram of Lyonesse* he speaks of "Sweet Love, that art so bitter," and in *Anactoria:*

My life is bitter with thy love; thine eyes
Blind me, thy tresses burn me . . .

His poems have many Sapphic echoes. In his youth he poured several of Sappho's fragments into the melting pot of *Anactoria*, where she is

[208]

a nerve-racked woman, torn by passion, sensuous and lascivious, altogether too "Sapphic." The rhetoric in his lines is gorgeous, but he loses much of Sappho's emotional power. "That one low, pellucid phrase," as Mackail calls the line, "I say that one will think of us even hereafter," is expanded into:

Yea, thou shalt be forgotten like spilt wine
Except these kisses of my lips on thine
Brand them with immortality; but me —
Men shall not see bright fire nor hear the sea,
Nor mix their hearts with music, nor behold
Cast forth of heaven with feet of awful gold
And plumeless wings that make the bright air blind,
Lightning, with thunder for a hound behind
Hunting through fields unfurrowed and unsown —
But in the light and laughter, in the moan
And music, and in grasp of lip and hand
And shudder of water that makes felt on land
The immeasurable tremor of all the sea,
Memories shall mix and metaphors of me.

The famous fragment of four lines which we have quoted above (p. 69) becomes:

Thee too the years shall cover; thou shalt be
As the rose born of one same blood with thee,
As a song sung, as a word said, and fall
Flower-wise, and be not any more at all,

Nor any memory of thee anywhere;
For never Muse has bound above thine hair
The high Pierian flower whose graft outgrows
All Summer kinship of the mortal rose
And colour of deciduous days, nor shed
Reflex and flush of heaven above thine head, etc.

The Aphrodite hymn which he paraphrased in
Anactoria is used again in *Songs of the Spring-
tides:*

O *thou of divers-coloured mind, O thou*
Deathless, God's daughter subtle-souled

. . . .

Child of God, close craftswoman, I beseech thee;
Bid not ache nor agony break nor master,
        Lady, my spirit.

(On the Cliffs)

In the same poem the mature Swinburne comes
closer than in his youth to Sappho, when he
says: "The tawny sweet-winged thing, Whose
cry was but of spring." But even in this poem
he dilutes Sappho's one line into six or more:

'I *loved thee'* — *hark, one tenderer note than all* —
'*Atthis, of old time once'* — *one low long fall,*
Sighing — *one long low lovely loveless call,*
Dying — *one pause in song so flamelike fast* —
'*Atthis, long since in old time overpast'* —
One soft first pause and last.

[210]

We cannot take leave of Swinburne without paying tribute to his Sapphics. English and American poets in general have not been successful with the Sapphic strophe, though in modern times Canning's *Needy Knife-grinder* is a good specimen; and Tennyson caught the real Greek cadence in his specimen:

> *Faded every violet, all the roses;*
> *Gone the glorious promise, and the victim*
> *Broken in this anger of Aphrodite*
> *Yields to the victor.*

Many have experimented with the Sapphic stanza, as recently Clinton Scollard and Thomas S. Jones, Jr., in their *Sapphics.*

TO A HILL–TOWN
(Last two stanzas)

Sighing winds and crooning of gentle waters;
Ilex boughs that tremble with tender music, —
Nightingales that sing in the scented gloaming, —
These for thee, Sappho!

Immortelles and chaplets of crimson roses, —
Roses loved of thee and beloved of Lesbos, —
Plaintive notes of lyres and the tears of lovers,
These for thee, Sappho!

(T. S. J.)

TO THE LESBIAN

You, *who first unloosed from the winds their burden*
On that lyre of magical trembling heart-strings,
Merged within all sorrow and human gladness —
So sang for all time:

Do you never still through the drifting shadows
Seek unseen the ways that you loved in Lesbos, —
Or alone for song's everlasting splendor
Were you made mortal?

(T. S. J.)

Sara Teasdale .(Mrs. Filsinger), who has been called one of the best of contemporary lyric poets and who is an ardent admirer of Sappho, has written the following striking lyric in the Sapphic stanza:

THE LAMP

If *I can bear your love like a lamp before me,*
When I go down the long steep Road of Darkness,
I shall not fear the everlasting shadows,
    Nor cry in terror.

If I can find out God, then I shall find Him;
If none can find Him, then I shall sleep soundly,
Knowing how well on earth your love sufficed me,
    A lamp in darkness.

Marion Mills Miller [182] has written some good Sapphics, though his theory of the proper ren-

dition of Sapphic metre will cause some controversy among scholars. We have not the space
here to discuss the history of the Sapphic metre,
which if not first used by Sappho was first perfected by her. It has been employed extensively
in all ages. Horace has it some twenty-six times.
Elizabethan renderings can be found in Robinson Ellis' preface to his translation of Catullus.
By Rhabanus (766–856) it was fitted to hymns
such as those for the *Feast of St. John the Baptist*,
for Candlemas, Michaelmas, and for the Feast
of St. Benedict, and it was employed for his
hymns in the *Common of Confessors* and the
Common of Virgins. But no one else has ever
caught the Sapphic rhythm and melody so well
as Swinburne in his early poem called *Sapphics:*

ALL *the night sleep came not upon my eyelids,*
S*hed not dew, nor shook nor unclosed a feather,*
Y*et with lips shut close and with eyes of iron*
  S*tood and beheld me.*

  .   .   .   .

  S*aw the reluctant*
F*eet, the straining plumes of the doves that drew her,*
Looking always, looking with necks reverted,
B*ack to Lesbos, back to the hills whereunder*
  S*hone Mitylene;*

  .   .   .   .

Ah the singing, ah the delight, the passion!
All the Loves wept, listening; sick with anguish,
Stood the crowned nine Muses about Apollo;
    Fear was upon them,

While the tenth sang wonderful things they knew not.
Ah the tenth, the Lesbian! the nine were silent,
None endured the sound of her song for weeping;
    Laurel by laurel.

Faded all their crowns; but about her forehead,
Round her woven tresses and ashen temples
White as dead snow, paler than grass in summer,
    Ravaged with kisses,

Shone a light of fire as a crown for ever.
Yea, almost the implacable Aphrodite
Paused, and almost wept; such a song was that song,
    Yea, by her name too

Called her, saying, 'Turn to me, O my Sappho;'
Yet she turned her face from the Loves, she saw not
Tears for laughter darken immortal eyelids,
    Heard not about her

.   .   .   .

Clothed about with flame and with tears, and singing
Songs that move the heart of the shaken heaven,
Songs that break the heart of the earth with pity,
    Hearing, to hear them.

AMERICAN. In America in early days little attention was paid to the content of Sappho, but the Phaon story is sometimes used, as for example by Philip Freneau of New Jersey, the "poet of the American Revolution," the "creature of the opposition" (1752–1832). In *The Monument of Phaon*, a poem published in 1795, in the form of a dialogue between Sappho and the traveller, Ismenius informs her that he saw the tomb of her deserter, Phaon, in Sicily, erected by another lady:

> *Not distant far a monument arose*
> *Among the trees, and form'd of Parian stone,*
>
> .   .   .   .
>
> *A sculptured Venus on the summit wept,*
> *A pensive Cupid dropt the parting tear.*

The last lines are:

I'll go! and from the high Leucadian steep
Take my last farewell in the lover's leap,
I charge thee Phaon, by this deed of woe,
To meet me in the Elysian shades below,
No rival beauty shall pretend a share,
Sappho alone shall walk with Phaon there.
She spoke, and downward from the mountain's
        height
Plung'd in the plashy wave to everlasting night.

Edgar Allan Poe (1809–1849) in the index to the first volume of the *Southern Literary Messenger* states that a stanza of Sappho's second ode is embodied in his poem, *To Sarah:*

> *In such an hour when are forgot*
> *The World, its cares and my own lot*
> *Thou seemest then to be*
> *A gentle guarding spirit given*
> *To guide my wandering thoughts to heaven*
> *If they should stray from thee.*

In *Ulalume* there is a possible echo of fragment (E. 16):

> *In terror she spoke, letting sink her*
> *Wings till they trailed in the dust,*
> *In agony sobbed, letting sink her*
> *Plumes till they trailed in the dust.*

In *Al Aaraaf*, I, 43 ff., Poe says in a note that he is referring to Sappho in the lines:

> *. . . lilies such as rear'd the head*
> *On the fair Capo Deucato, and sprang*
> *So eagerly around about to hang*
> *Upon the flying footsteps — deep pride —*
> *Of her who lov'd a mortal — and so died.*

Dr. Thomas O. Mabbott of Columbia University has called my attention to the fact that Poe

published a version of Sappho's second ode by
Mary E. Hewitt in *Broadway Journal*, I, no. 24
(1845); that he knew "Udoch's" note (*Southern
Literary Messenger*, I, p. 454, April, 1835) where
there is a reference to the *Spectator*, no. 229;
and that the paper, *Some Ancient Greek Authors*,
signed P. in the *Southern Literary Messenger*
for April, 1836, where a conventional account of
Sappho is given, was probably written by Poe.

Later American literature, like that of other
countries, is full of the name of Sappho, even
if it does not show a profound knowledge of
the fragments of the actual Sappho. In any
case, such dramas and poems and novels reveal
the tremendous potentiality of her name. We
have referred to translations or adaptations by
Easby-Smith, Lucy Milburn, J. M. O'Hara, Bliss
Carman, Petersen, Storer, and Marion Mills
Miller. There have been renderings of individual
poems by Felton, Higginson, Gildersleeve,
Shorey, Lawton, Appleton, Whicher, Horton,
Drake, and others; the first ode has been well
rendered in the metre of the original by Professor
Appleton, Professor Fairclough, and others (cf.
pp. 47–52 above).[73] We cannot list here all the
American renderings of single songs or frag-
ments, although we have incidentally in this

book mentioned many such, and an abundance of references will be found in the notes. Nor can we give the titles of all the tragedies and poems which have been inspired by the name of Sappho. We select only a few of the more important. There is an interesting tragedy in five acts called *Sappho of Lesbos* by Mrs. Estelle Lewis ("Stella"), whom Edgar Allan Poe called "the rival of Sappho." The play was put on the stage in London in 1868 and afterwards was given on the Athenian stage in a modern Greek version. It reached a seventh edition. It should be credited to America, since Mrs. Lewis was Miss Anna Blanche Robinson, born near Baltimore in 1824. She translated Virgil's *Aeneid* when a mere schoolgirl, and afterwards married Mr. Lewis of Brooklyn, New York. She travelled much abroad, but returned to America, where she wrote some of the plays before she went to live in London in 1865. In 1876 was published Ellen Frothingham's translation of Grillparzer's *Sappho*. In 1900–1913 H. V. Sutherland wrote his *Sappho and Phaon*, and in 1907 was published Percy Mackaye's tragedy with the same title. Even when he was a student at Harvard, he wrote an entirely distinct lyric drama in

[218]

verse, entitled *Sappho, or Archilochus and Hipponax*, in which he himself acted with a gathering of Harvard and Wellesley students in January, 1896. Unfortunately this drama has not been published. The published play is written mostly in iambic pentameter blank verse, with a few lyrics and some trochaic and dactylic lines; there are also several excellent Sapphics. It has never been very successful on the stage, although the music given with it is still so popular that it has been recently published by Professor Stanley (cf. bibliography). In the prologue a manuscript of Sappho's poems is imagined to have been found in excavating the theatre of Varius at Herculaneum, just as Lucy Milburn, who lived in Lesbus for a while, pretended that she procured her poems from papyri which she had discovered in a metal case in the Orient. The scene of the tragedy is an olive grove on a promontory overlooking the Aegean Sea. In the first act we have Atthis betrothed to Larichus, and Anactoria deserted by Alcaeus for Sappho. Pittacus is one of Sappho's suitors who quarrels with Alcaeus and in trying to strike him hits the slave Phaon. In the second act Sappho releases Phaon from his yoke and they flee from

[219]

Alcaeus after Phaon has struck him with his spear. In the third act Phaon again strikes at Alcaeus, but this time hits his own boy. Thalassa, his wife, shows him his own dead child and so he returns to her, and the rejected Sappho springs into the misty sea. There are inappropriate prose interludes with a pantomime of the drunken Hercules. Sappho is here again not the real Sappho but the Sappho of tradition, which is rather strange, as several of Sappho's fragments, by no means all that might have been suitable, are accurately and charmingly paraphrased. This shows that Mackaye knew the fragments of Sappho, but he has no real understanding of Sappho herself, for his Sappho is given to unrestrained love and she rejects a great poet and statesman for the married slave into whom Mackaye has transformed Phaon. I can quote only the very dramatic hymn to Poseidon and Aphrodite:

> GOD *of the generations, pain, and death,*
> I *bow to thee. Not for love's sake is love's*
> *Fierce happiness, but for the after-race.*
> Y*et, thou eternal Watcher of the tides,*
> *Knowing their passions, tell me! Why must we*
> R*apturous beings of the spray and storm*
> T*hat, chanting, beat our hearts against thy shores*

Of aspiration — ebb? ebb and return
Into the songless deep? are we no more
Than foam upon thy garment?

Another wave has broken at your feet
And, moaning, wanes into oblivion.
But not its radiance. That flashes back
Into the morning, and shall flame again
Over a myriad waves. That flame am I,
Nor thou, Poseidon, shalt extinguish me.
My spirit is thy changeling, and returns
To her, who glows beyond the stars of birth —
To her, who is herself time's passion star.

Many individual American poems have also
taken the title or themes from Sappho. Oliver
Wendell Holmes refers to her in the fourth
stanza of *The Voiceless:*

> *Not where Leucadian breezes sweep*
> *O'er Sappho's memory-haunted billow,*
> *But where the glistening night-dews weep*
> *On nameless sorrow's churchyard pillow.*
> (*The Atlantic Monthly,* Oct. 1858)

Samuel Latham Mitchill (1764–1831) reflects
Sappho's love of the rose in an imaginary dialogue between Sappho and her younger contemporary from Samos, Pythagoras:

PYTHAGORAS AND SAPPHO,
or
THE DIAMOND AND THE ROSE

LONG *time ago, 'tis well expressed,*
    Pythagoras the seer
This question artfully addressed
    To beauteous Sappho's ear:

"When hence thou shalt be forced to flee,
    By transmigration's power,
Wouldst thou indeed prefer to be
    A jewel *or a* flower?"

The Lesbian maid these words returned
    To greet the Samian sage,
"For gems my taste has never burned,
    And flowers my choice engage.

"The glittering stones, though rich and rare,
    No animation know,
While vegetables fine and fair
    With vital action glow.

"The senseless gem no pleasure moves,
    Displayed in fashion's use,
But flowers enjoy their gentle loves,
    And progeny produce.

"Then when I shall surmount," she cried,
    "Rude dissolution's storm,

Oh! let me not be petrified,
  But wear a living form.

"*Those matchless rays the diamond shows,*
  With promptness I decline,
That I may dwell within the rose
  And make its blossoms mine."

In recent years many poems have appeared on
Sappho. For example, thinking perhaps of the
story that Solon asked his nephew to teach him
a song of Sappho before he died, and echoing
the epithet of "sweetly smiling" in Alcaeus'
fragment, Richard Hovey (1864–1900) wrote in
The Independent, April 30, 1896, *A Dream of
Sappho:*

I DREAMED *of Sappho on a summer night,*
Her nightingales were singing in the trees
Beside the castled river; and the wind
Fell like a woman's fingers on my cheek,
And then I slept and dreamed and marked no change;
The night went on with me into my dream,
This only I remember, that I said:
'*O Sappho! ere I leave this paradise,*
Sing me one song of those lost books of yours
For which we poets still go sorrowing;
That when I meet my fellows on the earth
I may rejoice them more than many pearls;'

[223]

And she, the sweetly-smiling, answered me,
As one who dreams: 'I have forgotten them.'

We have referred above to Gamaliel Bradford's use of Sappho's apple on the topmost bough; and Maurice Thompson, the author of *Alice of Old Vincennes* and the *Sapphic Secret*, published as his last song, *Sappho's Apple* in *The Independent*, Feb. 21, 1901:

SAPPHO'S APPLE

A DREAMY *languor lapsed along,*
  And stirred the dusky-bannered boughs;
With half a sigh and half a song
  The crooning tree did nod and drowse,
While far aloft blush-tinted hung
  One perfect apple maiden-sweet,
At which the gatherers vainly flung,
  And could not get to hoard or eat.

"Reddest and best," they growled and went
  Slowly away, each with his load
Fragrant upon his shoulders bent,
  The hill-flowers darkening where they trode;
"Reddest and best; but not for us;
  Some loafing lout will see it fall;
The laborer's prize — 'twas ever thus —
  Is his who never works at all!"

[224]

Soon came a vagrant, loitering,
His young face browned by wind and sun,
Weary, yet blithe and prone to sing,
Tramping his way to Avalon;
Even I it was, who, long athirst
And hungry, saw the apple shine;
Then wondrous wild sweet singing burst
Flame-like across these lips of mine.

"O, ruby-flushed and flaring gold,
Thou splendid lone one left for me,
Apple of love to filch and hold,
Fruit-glory of a kingly tree!
Drop, drop into my hand,
That I may hide thee in my breast,
And bear thee far o'er sea and land,
A captive, to the purple West."

Renée Vivien (1877–1909), an American poetess of great promise who died all too young and all too unknown to students of Sappho (see bibliography), made some very nice French verse translations of Sappho which were published under a pseudonym in 1903 and reprinted anonymously in 1909. She pays her tribute to Sappho in these two verses:

Les siècles attentifs se penchent pour entendre
Les lambeaux de tes chants . . . . .

The Maryland poet, Father John B. Tabb, the
only American who with Emerson was admitted
to the Oxford *Garland Series on Epigrams*, has
two poems on Sappho, in the first of which
Keats is appropriately classed with Sappho:[183]

KEATS — SAPPHO

METHINKS, *when first the nightingale*
  Was mated to thy deathless song,
That Sappho with emotion pale,
  Amid the Olympian throng,
Again, as in the Lesbian grove,
  Stood listening with lips apart,
To hear in thy melodious love
  The pantings of her heart.

SAPPHO

A LIGHT *upon the headland, flaming far,*
  We see thee o'er the widening waves of time,
Impassioned as a palpitating star,
  Big with prophetic destiny sublime:
A momentary flash — a burst of song —
  Then silence, and a withering blank of pain.
We wait, alas! in tedious vigils long,
  The meteor-gleam that cometh not again!
Our eyes are heavy, and our visage wan:
  Our breath — a phantom of the darkness — glides

[226]

Ghostlike to swell the dismal caravan
  Of shadows, where thy lingering splendor hides,
Till, with our tears and ineffectual sighs,
  We quench the spark a smouldering hope supplies.

We have already referred to Alan Seeger's use of the famous midnight fragment (p. 78). The magazines are fond of the subject of Sappho and Phaon and have countless poems which refer to Phaon and the Leucadian Leap. Buchanan has a poem called *The Leucadian Rock;* and Edward J. O'Brien in the *Liberator* says:

Stir not the grasses here,
O wandering zephyr,
For Phaon travelled far over alien foam
Before his footsteps turned in soft contentment
Home to the green threshold
He had forgotten.

Sara Teasdale, the modern burning American Sappho, has a poem on *Phaon and the Leucadian Leap* in *Scribner's Magazine*, for December, 1913, pp. 725–6. The poem is too long to quote entire, and I can give only a few lines:

FAREWELL; across the threshold many feet
Shall pass, but never Sappho's feet again.

. . . .

'Whither goes Sappho lonely in the night?'
Whither goes Sappho? Whither all men go,
But they go driven, straining back with fear,
And Sappho goes as lightly as a leaf
Blown from brown autumn forests to the sea.

. . . . . .

Yet they shall say: 'It was for Cercolas —
She died because she could not bear her love.'

. . . . . .

Others shall say: 'Grave Dica wrought her death.'

. . . . . .

Ah, Dica, it is not for thee I go.
And not for Phaon, tho' his ship lifts sail
Here in the windless harbor, for the south.

. . . . . .

How should they know that Sappho lived and died
Faithful to love, not faithful to the lover,

. . . . . .

The gods have given life, I gave them song;
The debt is paid and now I turn to go.

Alfred Noyes, in his poem *In Memory of
Swinburne* uses the fragment which Swinburne
himself expanded (cf. p. 12). Edwin Arlington
Robinson [184] has translated *The Dust of Timas*
(cf. p. 100), which has recently been diluted
by William Stebbing into twelve verses in his
poem, *A Bride in Death*. Robinson's rendering

of Posidippus' epigram on Doricha is also excellent:

> SO NOW *the very bones of you are gone*
> W*here they were dust and ashes long ago;*
> *And there was the last ribbon you tied on*
> T*o bind your hair, and that is dust also;*
> *And somewhere there is dust that was of old*
> A *soft and scented garment that you wore —*
> T*he same that once till dawn did closely fold*
> Y*ou in with fair Charaxus, fair no more.*
>
> B*ut Sappho, and the white leaves of her song,*
> W*ill make your name a word for all to learn,*
> *And all to love thereafter, even while*
> I*t's but a name; and this will be as long*
> A*s there are distant ships that will return*
> *Again to your Naucratis and the Nile.*

There is little of Sappho except in name in Agnes Kendrick Gray's verses [185] or in those of William Alexander Percy.[186] Harry Kemp is thinking of Byron rather than Sappho herself when he says that the lines, "the Isles of Greece where burning Sappho loved and sung," went to his soul like a white hot iron. There is more in George Horton,[187] who in the last poem on Sappho which I have seen from his pen has a refrain on "bitter-sweet." Mr. Horton forgets that we do know that Pittacus, (see illustration (Pl. 2) was "lord of Lesbos' isle," but the general sentiment is true all the same:

BALLADE OF SAPPHO'S FAME

OH, WHO *was lord of Lesbos' isle*
When Sappho sang for many a year,
And great Apollo's self the while,
Ceased from the lyre and bent to hear?
The titles to his heart so near,
His lineage, who can now repeat?
Yet she escaped oblivion drear
Who said that love is "bitter-sweet."

And who by wealth or selfish guile
Became the island's proudest peer?
What siren with voluptuous wile
Was potent at the royal ear?
Who gained renown with sword and spear?
Their fame is dust beneath the feet
Of Time, and she alone is dear
Who said that love is "bitter-sweet."

Our joy is sadder than the smile
Of grief that cannot shed a tear;
Our lives are like a little mile
Marked on the orbit of a sphere;
The wisdom that we most revere
Is mixed with folly and defeat:

[230]

Her laurel never can grow sere
Who said that love is "bitter-sweet."

ENVOI

From out that pallid atmosphere
Where dawn and darkness vaguely meet,
Comes but her lark-note cool and clear
Who said that love is "bitter-sweet."

I have quoted enough to discredit "The King of the Black Isles" who in the *Line O'Type* of the *Chicago Tribune* for November, 1922, publishes a poem with the alliterative caption, *A Lady Lived in Lesbos.*[188] The last of the three stanzas is:

We have forgotten beauty and all our goods are good,
And little we remember now the dryads and the wood,
And only old philosophers and foolish dreamers know
What lady lived in Lesbos a weary time ago.

Even as this book goes to press, Tristram Tupper issues his novel, *Adventuring* (Doran Co., N. Y., 1923), in which Sappho is discovered even down in the valley of the Shenandoah:

"On such a night Jay Singleton discovered the most beloved singer of all the ages. Not in the Lesbian starlit dusk, nor yet in the golden-sandaled dawn, but beneath a smoky lamp in the valley of the Shenandoah. Found her in a book. And he

[231]

liked the cut of her verses — three pentameters
followed by a dipody; and he liked the cut of her
clothes — sort of loose and careless before the
Christian era. 'No use falling in love,' said Jay
Singleton to himself. 'She sang her songs six
hundred years B.C.'

"But he pored over another fragment, translated
another quatrain, looked up each word, strung
them together, made a kind of rime. In a word,
Jay Singleton tried to improve a bit on the inimitable Sappho. And that night out on his porch
where no one could hear, not even at the post
office quarter of a mile away, he struck the strings
of his guitar and he sang this surprising Sapphic:

Man is peer of gods in those moments after
Love has silenced song and has banished laughter;
Then — to her who smiles at him softly through
        tears —
    He has no peers.

"He laid aside his guitar and lit his pipe, that
made a pink glow in the darkness. He tried to
form in his mind an image of Sappho and of her
Isle of Lesbos, tried to wander back through the
labyrinthine ages, ages misty with music, dusky
with gold, red with wars, and blushing with roses —
forgotten wars, faded roses mingling to form the
perfume of the centuries. He pulled on his pipe.
'Where is she now?' Easy enough to imagine
Sappho with her ivory throat, her violet eyes and
sandals of golden dawn, back in the golden dawn
of poetry. For, overhead, these were her stars.
But he wondered about the form her singing soul
had taken after she had leaped into the Ionian Sea.

Had the waters quenched the spark, or was her soul immortal — a flame that twenty-five hundred years had failed to extinguish? Again he asked: 'Where are you now? Where in this, the most cluttered up of all the ages?' He tried to imagine her beside the Little Calfpasture — Sappho beside the Calfpasture Creek, sighing, laughing, singing her lyrics! 'No use falling in love! Sang your songs twenty-five hundred years ago!'"

In May, 1922, Miss Bertha Bennett of Carleton College produced an interesting pageant "A Grecian Festival" on the Sappho and Phaon story, with adaptations of Sappho's first two odes and representing Sappho as leaping into Lyman lake. It ends with the union of Sappho and Phaon, after death, on Mt. Olympus.

AN ADDENDUM ON SAPPHO IN RUSSIAN

Many Russian writers mention Sappho, especially Vyacheslav Ivanov; and in a volume republished in Berlin, 1923, (*Zovy Drevnosti, Echoes of the Past*) Konstantin Dmitriyevich Balmont has translated eight of Sappho's fragments. The same poet (*Zacharovanny Grot, The Enchanted Grotto*, vol. III, 1908) has published a poem on Sappho which my former student, now of Columbia University, Dr. Clarence Manning, has translated in the original metre:

> O *Sappho, thou dost know alone*
> How hard the poet strives revealing
> The secrets beauty once has shown
> In moments of immortal feeling.
>
> O *Sappho, thou dost know alone* —
> Thy name a perfume's sweetness holy —
> The dreams that we one day have known
> But lost unspoken, faded wholly.
>
> O *Sappho, thou dost know alone*
> How clearly in uncounted masses
> Still unreached flowers yet are grown
> Where life through the charmed grotto passes.

XII. SAPPHO'S INFLUENCE ON MUSIC

ON THE operatic stage Sappho has had much influence; and above I have told how Lamartine said that Sappho was a superb subject for an opera, although he never wrote the opera, and how Grillparzer was asked to write an opera on Sappho. In French we have a lyrical tragedy, *Sapho*, by Empis and Courniol (1818), Delavault's *Sapho* and Gounod's *Sapho* (1851); and a few years ago (1897) Massenet produced his *Sapho*. In Italian there is Pacini's *Saffo* (Naples 1840); in Dutch, Bree's *Sapho;* in German, Schwartzendorf's *Sappho* and Kanne's *Sappho;* in Bohemian, there is Reicha's *Sappho;* and in Russian, Lissenko's *Sappho*.

Brahms composed a *Sapphic Ode*, which is very familiar because it is often sung to-day and there is an English victrola record of it by Julia Clausen, but while it deals with Sappho's favorite flower, the rose, it is Sapphic only in name and metre:

Rosen brach ich nachts mir am dunklen Hage.
Süsser hauchten Duft sie, als je am Tage;

[234]

Doch verstreuten reich die bewegten Aeste
Thau, der mich nässte
Auch der Küsse Duft mich wie nie berüchte,
Die ich nachts von Strauch deiner Lippen pflückte;
Doch auch dir bewegt ein Gemüth gleich jenen,
Thauten die Thränen.

(Words by HANS SCHMIDT)

From the time of the *Schemata Musica* printed in Volger's edition of 1810, down to the music published by G. Cipollini in 1890 in his brother's *Saffo*, many have put Sappho's songs to music. Even in the last few years many have tried their hand at the task. Perhaps the most successful music, with a real touch of the old Greek flavor, is that which was composed by Professor Stanley for several of Sappho's fragments in connection with Mr. Harrison Grey Fiske's stage presentation of Percy Mackaye's *Sappho and Phaon*. This has been reprinted this year in a general treatment of Greek music by Professor Stanley of the University of Michigan. The selections published include " Builders, Build the Roof-Beam High, Hymenaeon"; "Gath'rers, What Have We Forgot, Hymenaeon!"; "What shall we do, Cytherea?"; "Hollow Shell, Horny Shell"; "Akoue, Poseidon"; "Hesper, Eleleu", etc. Miss Pearl C. Wilson, of Miss Chandor's

School in New York, a former student of Professor Perry of Columbia University, without making any pretense of reproducing the ancient music has composed musical accompaniments for several of the odes and also of the new fragments, which have been sung with much success. She tried to illustrate the metre of each fragment, but found it more satisfactory to write the music without the modern division into bars and rests, simply indicating the long and short syllables by notes of different values. This makes possible a lyric delivery of the poems, each line determined solely by the words and their meaning. In that way the simple melodies as expressions of the thought gain a great deal when sung. I can testify from my own public experiments in readings from Sappho that her fragments can be much better recited or chanted when accompanied by music, as I am convinced they were originally.

XIII. EPILOGUE AND CONCLUSION

I VENTURE to hope that out of all I have written in the preceding pages some fairly clear idea of Sappho may have emerged. Yet the discussion has had to wander widely through literature which has, indeed, been influenced strongly by her name but journeys far from the Lesbian lyrist herself. In closing this study it may be well, therefore, to return to the woman and the poet and add some final words.

The fragments of many other ancient poets have been collected for merely scholastic reasons, but Sappho's literary remains are more than antique specimens. They constitute a great and noble literature and some of the latest found are among the best. They often rank as highly as the completed poems of other writers — surely an unparalleled phenomenon. In them we recognize the creator's genius as clearly as in a fragmentary torso of Phidias we see the sculptor's art in every chiselled line. While we miss the fullness of her life, we can restore her

figure because the fragments are "the real blood
of her heart and the real flame of her thought."
Nearly every line of them has been imitated,
dilated or diluted, and, disgraceful to say, many
who have drunk of her living water have
poisoned it into stagnant and salacious slime.
There is nothing like this in the history of literature. Higginson in 1871 summarized the case:

"What other woman played such a part in
moulding the great literature that has moulded the
world? Colonel Mure thinks that a hundred such
women might have demoralized all Greece. But
it grew demoralized at any rate; and even the
island where Sappho taught took its share in the
degradation. If, on the other hand, the view taken
of her by more careful criticism be correct, a hundred such women might have done much to save
it. Modern nations must again take up the problem where Athens failed and Lesbos only pointed
the way to the solution, — to create a civilization
where the highest culture shall be extended to
woman also. It is not enough that we should dream,
with Plato, of a republic where man is free and
woman but a serf. The aspirations of modern life
culminate, like the greatest of modern poems, in
the elevation of womanhood. 'Die ewige Weibliche
zieht uns hinan.'"

Sappho, then, was a pure and good woman,
busily and successfully engaged in the work of
her chosen profession. She was a teacher of

[238]

singing and dancing and the technique of poetry, and to give her pupils the finest models she applied herself so seriously to the lyric art that she reached a perfection in it to which no other classic poet attained. If she ever collected her verse it was only to promote the idealization of marriage pageants, and not with the purpose of publishing a full edition of her songs. It would not be safe to deny that there was a practically useful collection of Sappho's songs in the archives of her school or guild or in the Temple of Aphrodite, but no copies were sold at the bookstalls in her own day as certainly was later the case in fifth century Athens.

Sappho, in fact, must be listed with two other names which, taken together, form a unique and astonishing group, a group whose peculiar and distinguishing feature is that their enduring thoughts and imperishable words were indispensable necessities in their life-work rather than productions as literature for the sake of literature. It is not because of the accidental alliteration that we rank Sappho with Socrates and Shakespeare. These great exemplars of song, ethics, and drama, respectively, were alike in that it was not by their intention that their works became literature. Shakespeare as a theatrical manager was obliged by his position to write plays that would attract audiences. He was compelled by his genius to make those dramas imperishable. But if he had had his way none of them would ever have been printed. Our gratitude must be given to prompters' copies and to literary thieves. Socrates was a teacher whose purely oral lessons his pupils, Plato and Xenophon, committed to writing that the master's inspiring thoughts might not die.

Socrates' love for his young disciples was a love passing the love of women. The myriad-minded man of Stratford, — "Gentle Will," as his comrades called him, — had an affectionate sympathy with all sorts and conditions of his fellow-men. Sappho's love for her girl friends was so intense that there are those who, not knowing how passionate the love of woman can be for woman, still fail, despite the evidence, to recognize a love more sublime even than that for man.

How jealous she could be of her family's good name! More than once she prays that no dishonor may come to her house. How jealous also of those who sought to win away the love of her girls and of the girls themselves when any of them seemed to have forgotten her! How intensely, too, she could hate, the outbursting passion against the "she-dog" at the close of fragment E 36, which we have translated on page 20, may serve to suggest. The fierceness of her satire is also incidentally shown in this as well as in other fragments. (See E 35, 37, 71, *et al.*)

Like Socrates and Shakespeare Sappho had a planetary mind swinging in its orbit with ease through all realms, whether of nature, or human nature, or the divine nature of the unseen world. This need not be elaborated here, save in Sappho's case. But it may be worth while to repeat some of the evidence as to Sappho's wide range of thought as it is seen in a few typical instances. She loved the roses, the clover, and the anthrysc. She loved the doves and the nightingales, and knew their colorings and discerned their ways. But the unplucked apple on the top of the topmost bough, the myriad ears of the listening night that hears what the girl across the sea says and relays it right over the waves, the rosy-fingered moon well above the horizon and launching light across the rolling sea and over the fields of flowers, reveal even in the fragments which are "small but

[241]

roses," how surpassing were her instincts for nature's loftier meanings as well as its minute details and how exquisite were her comparisons. As for the phases of love — they were her daily business, — and each new couple whose wedding festivities she arranged in song gave her new material. Where in all literature is there a finer example of the union of human love along with insight into the soul of nature than in the ode, *To Absent Anactoria?* (See p.72)

As we have said, she knew the heart of the Greek bride and her dread at the loss of her free virginity. Mother love, too, was never more exquisitely portrayed than in the song we have quoted on pp. 27–28. But the subject of woman's love for woman is peculiarly her own. The finest lines in all Sappho's poetry are those descriptive of Anactoria in a poem which we might call *Old Love is Best* (E. 38, pp. 82–83 above).

Finished style, the γλαφυρὸς χαρακτήρ, as the Greek critics called it, simple purity but effective luminosity and exquisite rarity of expression, faultless constraint, fine taste in choosing appropriate subjects, marvellous verbal economy, comprehensive power in single words, fiery passion as well as austerity, richness and beauty, good arrangement of words, assonance, alliteration, consonantal harmonies, lingering vowel music and melody, produced often by the repetition of long vowels, the soft Aeolic quality of the Greek sounds, swift changes of nature and enchanting images, varied metres, but above all else, charm, that greatest characteristic of Sappho so emphasized by the ancients and moderns, — all these qualities she used that her songs and hymns might be perfect. It is this simple natural perfection of her art, like the "nothing too much" of the Parthenon frieze, that makes her untranslatable, even though it is precisely the quality which modern literature lacks but needs. Her nature was so great and her genius so marvellous and her purposes so inexorable that, in attending with her whole soul to her business as the poetic and musical caterer for successive weddings upon an ancient and interesting island, she incidentally made word-music and created thought-images which sounded the depths and scaled the heights of human passion and which winged their way to distant shores. The strains of her songs are beginning to be heard everywhere and are ever growing clearer and sweeter in this present timely century, the century of

woman's exaltation and glorification. Her
genius is concisely summed up by Watts-Dunton
in his *Essay on Poetry*, as follows: "*Never before
these songs were sung, and never since, did the
human soul, in the grip of a fiery passion, utter
a cry like hers; and, from the executive point of
view, in directness, in lucidity, in that high, im-
perious verbal economy which only nature can
teach the artist, she has no equal, and none worthy
to take the place of second.*"

In the Lesbus and the Asia Minor of Sappho's
day as in those of Homer, women were at their
zenith and were allowed greater freedom in life
and speech than in later Athens where woman's
position had reached its nadir, even though
literature and art had attained their highest
bloom. In Athens women were cabin'd, cribb'd,
confined. The more ancient Greeks in general,
however, even if their law made the wife the
property of her lord and master, appreciated
their women and considered them close to the
divine, else they would not have appointed them
to important priesthoods and other offices and
to be interpreters of the desires of the gods and
counsellors of their own political troubles.
Sappho was a twentieth century woman living
in sixth century Lesbus, who could go about

town without a chaperon and take part in the most intellectual and religious meetings. Of course she was "ni une sainte ni surtout une prude," as Reinach says. Rarely is a woman who is interesting a "saint." Reinach compares her also to Madame de Sévigné, who wrote to her daughter "paroles de feu et de fièvre . . . tout pareils à ceux de l'amour." What with her teaching, with her own writings, and with the executive work of the *hetairiai*, those ancient Y. W. C. A.'s for the cultivation of poetry and music, which Mackail has so aptly compared with the Courts of Love which existed in Languedoc from the twelfth to the fourteenth century, she was too noble and too busy to be devoted to ignobler ways, falsely ascribed to her. But her love was deeper than that of the schoolgirl in convent, conservatory of music, or literary club. She was no Ruskin-like school-mistress presiding over a group of virtuous but bold young women. She was respectable and respected. There was in her sacred guild under the patronage of Aphrodite "l'étroite et tendre intimité de jeunes filles de bonne naissance entre elles et avec leurs dirigeantes" (Reinach). But we utterly reject today the Athenian vaudeville idea of

Sappho, who never should have been branded a courtesan.

How the fine radiance Sappho shed on woman's love for woman and on her love of love and on the glory of pure and honorable marriage shines at last across these twenty-five hundred years! Her figure stands there on her isle. In itself it is white marble veined with gold. Much mud from many lands has been flung against it. For centuries, almost for millenniums, it has been soiled and stained. Even good men have come to think of the stains as integral parts of the statue, and of the gold as base metal. But the winds and rains of time have tired out the soilers and washed the figure white and clean of all Attic and all later defilings. It is all pure marble now, veined with warm gold. Something that suggests the Pygmalion miracle is happening to it. The statue is alive and luminous with its own beauty, grace, and power. Sappho's poetry deals with the eternal experiences of the human heart and carries with it those touches which make the whole world kin. As T. G. Tucker says: "Love and Sorrow are re-born with every human being. Time and civilisation make little difference."

EPILOGUE AND CONCLUSION

And not unhallowed was the page
By wingèd Love inscribed, to assuage
The pangs of vain pursuit;
Love listening while the Lesbian Maid
With finest touch of passion swayed
Her own Aeolian lute.

(WORDSWORTH, *Upon the Same Occasion*, 1819)

NOTES AND BIBLIOGRAPHY

NOTES

(The dates given in the text with authors are generally those of *floruit, i.e.* about the fortieth year.)

1. Somewhere recently in a newspaper I saw these lines entitled, *They Lived Too Soon:*

> *I fear Cleopatra was wasted*
> *Way back in her misty old realm.*
> *As matters befell, she did fairly well*
> *But she'd have been great in a film.*
> *If Dido and Sappho were with us —*
> *They're advertised widely, you see —*
> *And Helen of Troy — good gracious*
> *My boy, what movie successes they'd be.*

2. *Oxyrhynchus Papyri*, XV. 1787, frag. 4.
3. Galen, *Protrep.*, 2.
4. *Classical Philology*, XVIII. 35 ff. (1923).
5. Sir Edward Cook, *More Literary Recreations*, 1919, p. 205, quotes Wharton with approval to the effect that Tennyson called Sappho "the poet, implying her supremacy by the absence of any added epithet."
6. *Anth. Pal.*, VII. 16.
7. Athenaeus, *Deipnosophistae* (Doctors at dinner), 596 b.
8. *Odes*, IV. 9. 11.
9. *Amatorius*, 18.
10. Athenaeus, 598 b.
11. *Loves*, 30.
12. Lord Neaves, *The Greek Anthology*, p. 113.
13. *Anth. Pal.*, VII. 15.
14. Fraenkel, *Inschriften von Pergamon*, I, p. 118, no. 198; *C. I. G.* 3555.
15. *Sappho und Simonides*, p. 41, 1.
16. *Anth. Pal.*, IX. 66.
17. *Anth. Pal.*, VII. 14.

18. *Anth. Pal.*, VII. 407.

19. *Anth. Pal.*, IX. 189. Cf. A. J. Butler, *Amaranth and Asphodel*, Oxford, 1922, p. 195. The ending is "you shall fain Deem that Calliope doth hymn the strain."

20. *Anth. Pal.*, IX. 571.

21. XXXV. 16.

22. Cf. also Epigr. LXX, Jacobs, II, p. 25; Plut., *Amat.*, XII, p. 42.

23. P. 186 (1921).

24. 280, pp. 817–818. Cf. also *Posthumous Essays* in *Sat. Rev.*, Feb. 21, 1914.

25. Professor Scribner in *The Classical Weekly* XV, 1921, p. 78, says "there still is room for a work giving a complete critical treatment of Sappho's influence on ancient and modern literature down to our own time."

26. Athenaeus, 599 c; *Oxyr. Pap.*, XV. 1800.

27. Strabo, 618; Athenaeus, 85 c.

28. Cf. Herodotus, II. 135; Schol. Plato, *Phaedrus*, 235 c; *Ox. Pap.*, XV. 1800. The papyrus gives Scamandrus, which is otherwise known as a good Lesbian name, as well as Scamandronymus. Scamandrus like Suidas' Scamon is an abbreviation or *Kosenamen*.

29. *Her.*, XV. 61.

30. Confirmed by the new papyrus. The more correct form would be Clévis (Κλεῦις or Κλεῖϊς) after the founder of Lesbus, who was named Κλεύας, Strabo, 582.

31. Cf. Edmonds, pp. 144–147.

32. Hiller von Gaertringen, *Inschriften von Priene*, 18; for Erygyius cf. also Diodorus, XVII. 81, 83; Arrian, III. 6, 5.

33. The name occurs as a love-name on the interior of an Attic cylix in the Metropolitan Museum of New York, signed by Hieron (480 B.C.), published in *American Journal of Archaeology*, XXVII. 274 (1923). Near a female figure dancing to the accompaniment of the double flute played by a satyr is the inscription, "Beautiful Rhodopis." Cf. also Lucian, *De Saltatione*, 2.

34. Cf. Poulsen, *Delphi*, London, 1920, pp. 31, 72, 205, 294.

35. Edmonds' first poetical translation is given in his

Sappho in the Added Light of the New Fragments, p. 8; but he gives a revised prose version in the *Classical Review*, XXXIV. 5–6 (1920) and in *Lyra Graeca*, I, p. 207.

36. Solmsen in *Rhein. Mus.*, LVI. 502, 1 (1901) gives arguments for the spelling with double p.

37. 599 c.

38. γέγονε often means flourished, not "was born." Those who put Sappho's birth as late as 610 forget this.

39. Strabo, 617, also makes Sappho contemporary with Pittacus and Alcaeus. Eusebius puts the *floruit* of Sappho in the first year of the forty-fifth Olympiad (599 B.C.). Edmonds, *Lyra Graeca*, I, p. 142, adopts the reading Ol. 45, 2 (598 B.C.), but this would be rather the date of her exile.

40. The abbreviation E, is used throughout for Edmonds, *Lyra Graeca*, vol. I.

41. Cf. Prinz, *Funde aus Naukratis*, 1906, pp. 57 ff.

42. II. 134.

43. In another fragment (E. 35) Edmonds calls Sappho "an old bird," but this is a very dubious restoration based on only three preserved letters.

44. *Flor.*, XXIX. 58.

45. Dioscorides in *Anth. Pal.*, VII. 407 has Eresus; and coins and Suidas give both towns. Cf. Wilamowitz, *Sappho und Simonides*, 23; Her. II. 135 and references in Jacoby, *Das Marmor Parium*, 1904, p. 101. Many sources call Sappho a Mytilenaean, Schol. to Pindar (E. p. 144); Schol. Plato, *Phaedrus*, 235 c; Arist., *Rhet.*, 1398 b; *Anth. Pal.*, VII. 17. Some scholars assume that there were two Sapphos, but the two traditions can easily be reconciled by supposing that Sappho belonged to both cities, born at Eresus but later living at Mytilene. Edmonds thinks that Strabo would have mentioned Sappho when he is speaking of Eresus (618), had he believed her to have been born there, but Strabo omits many famous writers. The tradition of two Sapphos is found also in Aelian, *Historical Miscellanies*, XII. 19 and in Suidas. Cf. the novel *Beulah* by Augusta Evans, pp. 216–218: "Do you think that Sappho's frenzy was established by the Leucadian leap? You confound the poetess with a Sappho, who lived later, and threw herself into the sea from the

promontory of Leucate. Doubtless she too had 'poetic idio-
syncrasies,' but her spotless life, and I believe natural death,
afford no indication of an unsound intellect."

46. *Studies of the Greek Poets*, vol. I., pp. 307 ff. (American
ed.)

47. I. 9.

48. Cf. *The Poet Loves of Sappho* from the third book of
A Catalogue of Things Relating to Love, an elegiac poem by
Hermesianax, translated by J. Bailey.

49. Athenaeus, 450 e.

50. *Class. Phil.*, XIII. 348 (1918).

51. XVIII. 9.

52. Edmonds, 82, p. 240.

53. *Oxyrhynchus Papyri*, XV, 1922, 1800. Also now published in Miller-Robinson, *The Songs of Sappho*.

54. Lunák, *Quaestiones Sapphicae*, Kazan, 1888.

55. Lucy Milburn, p. 21, makes Sappho say, "When Cleïs,
I called her for my mother, was two years old, I found myself a widow." But we have no such evidence, how old Cleïs
was when her father died. Miss Milburn (Letter XIX) is
also quite wrong in translating "I would rather have my
little daughter know her own worth than to bequeath to her
all the treasures of Lydia, were they mine."

56. I. 30.

57. Edmonds, 116 reads Εἰρήνα (peace) for Ἔραννα so
that it is doubtful if Erinna, the poetess who wrote poems
worthy of Homer before her early death at the age of nineteen,
is really meant by Sappho. Most scholars now date her long
after Sappho's time, some even as late as 350 B.C.

58. Cf. *Jahrbuch*, XXV. 150 (1910).

59. *A. J. P.*, XXXIV. 106 (1913).

60. *Anth. Pal.*, XVI. 310.

61. XVIII.

62. *Odes*, I. 1. 36.

63. Cf. *Anth. Pal.*, VII. 14 and 17 for epigrams about
Sappho's grave. Cf. Edmonds, 42 and 99. Tucker
translates:

> *As friends we'll part:*
> *Win thee a younger bride:*

Too old, I lack the heart
To keep thee at my side.

64. My late colleague and dear friend, Kirby Flower Smith, made a brilliant reconstruction of the story which he read several times in public. It is to be deeply regretted that the manuscript has never been printed. Cf. for the Menander fragment, F. G. Allinson's *Menander*, in *The Loeb Classical Library*, pp. 400–401. For fragments of Plato's *Phaon*, cf. Kock, *C. A. F.*, I, p. 645. Cf. Servius on Virgil, *Aeneid*, III. 274.

65. Lucian for example, *Dialogues of the Dead*, 9, has Phaon carry Aphrodite over in his boat from Chios.

66. *Incred.*, 49 in Apostolius, *Paroem.*, II. 707.

67. 596 b; "according to Nymphis in his *Voyage around Asia*, the courtesan of Eresus who was a namesake of the other Sappho and lover of the fair Phaon won great notoriety." Cf. also Suidas, s. v. *Phaon*.

68. Cf. Furtwängler-Reichhold, *Gr. Vas.*, pl. 59; Milani, *Monumenti scelti del R. Museo Arch. di Firenze*, pl. 3; Nicole, *Meidias*, pl. VI, I. Cf. also on Phaon, Wilamowitz, *Sappho und Simonides*, pp. 33 ff.

69. 69 d.

70. Strabo, 452.

71. Cf. Curtis, *A. J. A.*, XXIV. 146 ff. (1920); Paribeni, *Boll. d'Arte*, I. 104 (1921); F. Cumont, *Rassegna d'Arte*, VIII. 44 ff. (1921); Leopold, *Mélanges d'Archéologie et d'Histoire*, XXXIX. pl. II. 181 ff. (1921); *Le Musée Belge*, XXVII. 15 ff. (1923), there connected by Hubaux with the cult of the Thracian Cotyto. Cf. *Memoirs Am. Ac. in Rome*, IV. 85 f., pl. XLV.

72. For another version cf. G. Showerman's *Ovid* in *The Loeb Classical Library*. A new translation by Marion Mills Miller, where the narrative portions are in recitative and the frequent outbursts of emotion in lyrical form, appears in Miller-Robinson, *The Songs of Sappho*.

73. Countless translations have been made. Among a few, I mention Philips (1711), Herbert (1713), Akenside's paraphrase (1745), Fawkes (1760), Merivale (1833), Elton (1814), Egerton (1815), Edinburgh Review (1832), Palgrave

(1854), Arnold (1869), Higginson (1871), Walhouse (1877), Symonds (at least two versions), Swinburne, Thomas Davidson, Marion Mills Miller (in *The Classics* and also in his play *The Return of Odysseus*, p. 82), Appleton, Fairclough (*The Raven*, V, 1904, p. 120), Easby Smith, Stobart (*The Glory that was Greece*, p. 119), Lawton, Tucker, Petersen, Lawrence (*Classical Review*, XXXVI, 1922, p. 2), Edmonds, William A. Drake (*Sewanee Review*, April 1923).

74. στροῦθοι in l. 10 are birds of Venus, swans, or better doves, rather than the dirty chatterers of our city streets, who never appear in Greek art. Cf. Throop, *Wash. Univ. Studies*, IX 282 (1922); Aristophanes, *Lysistrata*, 723 f.; Statius, *Silvae*, I. 2. Edmonds p. 183 reads the dual and translates "thy two swans." For swans drawing Aphrodite's or Cupid's car, cf. Reinach, *Répertoire des Vases Peints*, I, pp. 57, 271.

75. *Dem.*, 38.

76. *Iliad*, X. 90–95. Cf. also *Od.*, XVII. 518–521. For Homer's influence on Sappho cf. Smyth, p. 230; H. L. Ebeling, in *The Classical Weekly*, XVI. 195 ff. (1923).

77. III. 152–158.

78. Edmonds, pp. 186–7, makes the ingenious but very uncertain suggestion that in line 7 a proper noun, Brocheo or Brochea, corresponding to Catullus' Lesbia, should be read and now translates: "When I look on you, Brocheo, my speech comes short or fails me quite." Formerly he thought that the poem was sent by the banished Sappho at the age of eighteen to some beloved girl friend soon after her arrival in Sicily in 596 B.C., but Sappho was older than eighteen in 596, and Edmonds now makes an entirely different emendation of the last line, "but now that I am poor, I must fain be content . . . " meaning "beggars can't be choosers." But the reading is uncertain and I do not believe that Sappho was poor, nor do I agree with Miss Patrick that the words do not describe love at all.

79. For such head-cloths cf. the Latin word *struppus* and the festival at Falerii, called *struppearia*, Dion. Hal., XI. 39 and Poulsen, *Etruscan Tomb Paintings*, p. 23. Edmonds' new reading is very uncertain; for his previous reading and

poetical version cf. *Sappho in the Added Light of the New Fragments*, p. 28.

80. I keep Bergk's reading, "Foolish woman, pride not thyself on a ring." Edmonds changes the text and translates, "But come, be not so proud of a ring."

81. Cf. Poulsen, in *Jahrbuch*, XXI. 209 ff. (1906); *Die Bronzen von Olympia*, IV., pl. VII. 74.

82. There are many other poetical versions by Merivale, Symonds, F. Tennyson, Tucker, Cox, Edmonds, etc. For an absurd interpretation *Sappho in the Rain*, cf. *Wiener Studien*, XXXVIII. 176 ff. (1916).

83. Poetical translations by Merivale, Arnold, Appleton, F. Tennyson, Symonds, Edmonds, Miller, Percy Mackaye, etc.

84. *Sappho in the Added Light of the New Fragments*, p. 25, but in *Lyra Graeca*, I, p. 253, he changes his previous emendation and reads a text which I consider very uncertain, "and pours down a sweet shrill song from beneath his wings, when the Sun-god illumines the earth with his downshed flame outspread."

85. *Praec. Con.*, 48; *Qu. Conv.*, III. 1. 2.

86. *Flor.*, IV. 12.

87. For Swinburne's expansion cf. p. 210; cf. also Percy Mackaye in *Sappho and Phaon*. Bliss Carman has evolved the following from Sappho's one line:

> *I loved thee, Atthis, in the long ago*
> *When the great oleanders were in flower*
> *In the broad herded meadows full of sun.*
> *And we would often at the fall of dusk*
> *Wander together by the silver stream,*
> *When the soft grass-heads were all wet with dew*
> *And purple misted in the fading light,*
> *And joy I knew and sorrow at thy voice,*
> *And the superb magnificence of love —*
> *The loneliness that saddens solitude,*
> *And the sweet speech that makes it durable,*
> *The bitter longing and the keen desire,*
> *The sweet companionship through quiet days*
> *In the slow ample beauty of the world*

> *And the unutterable glad release*
> *Within the temple of the holy night;*
> *O Atthis, how I loved thee long ago*
> *In that fair perished summer by the sea.*

88. Cf. Miss Shields, *"Lesbos in the Trojan War,"* in *The Classical Jour.*, XIII. 670 ff. (1918); *The Cults of Lesbos* (Johns Hopkins University Diss.) 1917.

89. Cf. *Transactions and Proceedings of the American Philological Association*, LIII. xvi (1922).

90. For Mnesidice Edmonds would now read Anactoria. There is a good metrical translation by G. M. Whicher in Manatt, *Aegean Days*, London, 1913, p. 286.

91. *Odes*, I. 3. 22.

92. O'Hara renders as follows:

> *Gold is the son of Zeus,*
> *Immortal, bright;*
> *Nor moth nor worm may eat it,*
> *Nor rust tarnish.*

> *So are the Muse's gifts*
> *The offspring fair,*
> *That merit from high heaven*
> *Youth eternal.*

93. These may be vases in the form of an *astragalus* or knuckle-bone, two or three of which in clay are to be seen in museums, or they may be bowls or cups with the bottom rounded like one end of a knuckle bone. They might be bowls with a mid-boss in the form of a knuckle-bone. For such gold-bossed golden bowls as Pollux (VI, 98) mentions in the context of this quotation see the recently acquired beautiful gold bowl with a Corinthian inscription of about Sappho's time in the Boston Museum, which, however, is probably a modern forgery. Cf. *Bulletin, Boston Museum of Fine Arts*, XX. 65 ff. (1922).

94. German and Austrian scholars have failed to see the lovely lyrical literature in this delightful ballad. Aly considers it only the beginning of a longer ode; and I cannot

agree with him that it does not fit in with what we know of
Sappho who often expresses her loneliness in the absence of
her companions. Even if the thought is of love, we must not
expect consistency in a high-strung Aeolian woman. Fragments such as E. 152, 159, 167 may have been in a totally
different context. But I do not mean to say that the ballad
certainly refers to Sappho herself. The context is gone and
it is not even definitely assigned to Sappho. Some of the
editions seem to have contained it, but much anonymous
literature has been included in the Sapphic *corpus* as in that
of Plato or Hippocrates. However, as it is one of the prettiest
and most perfect pieces and quite in Sappho's style and metre
and thought, I consider it genuine. Ovid (*Sappho to Phaon*,
155 ff.) seems to know the lines. Ruthlessly to insert a
negative in the text ("Alone I do not sleep") as does Lunák
(*Wiener Studien*, XL, 1918, p. 98) spoils the literary quality
and makes it insipid. How much suggestive concision in
those seventeen words in four verses (four of them small
particles), but what vast and profound humanity; silence,
solitude, obscurity, waiting, anxiety, sympathy of nature.
How the strong and rapid description catches our deepest
thoughts. Such things disprove the arguments against its
genuineness by Wilamowitz, *Textgeschichte*, p. 33; and *Sappho
und Simonides*, p. 75. Cf. Münscher, *Hermes*, LIV. 29, 4
(1919).

95. *Scribner's Magazine*, September 1905, p. 304.

96. On the whole tradition of the wedding song cf. Mangels-
dorff, *Das lyrische Hochzeitsgedicht bei den Griechen und Römern*,
1913; Reitzenstein, *Hermes*, XXXV. 95 ff. (1900); Croiset,
Journal des Savants, July 1914; Girard, *Le Mariage de Hector*,
Comptes-rendus Ac. des Sc. et Belles-lettres, 1914, pp. 658–9.

97. I. 4

98. Cf. Robinson, *The Classical Weekly*, V. 68 (1911).

99. In this account of Sappho's wedding-songs I am much
indebted to Koechly, *Akademische Vorträge und Reden*, Zürich,
1859, pp. 153–217.

100. For Usener's interesting conjecture about Lesbian
marriage customs based on this fragment cf. *Kleine Schriften*,
IV, pp. 308 ff.

101. An excellent modern musical version will be found in A. A. Stanley, *Greek Themes in Modern Musical Settings*.

102. For the history of dialogue in Greek epigrams and examples of stones speaking with the passer-by and for sepulchral symbolism as in the Pelagon epigram cf., D. M. Robinson, "Two Epitaphs from Sardis," in *Anatolian Studies presented to Sir William Mitchell Ramsay*, Manchester, 1923, pp. 341–353.

103. For a bronze in the British Museum supposed to represent the reclining Sappho cf. Walters, *Cat. of Bronzes*, London, 1899, 203.

104. Pollux, IX. 84.

105. Cf. Bernoulli, *Griechische Ikonographie*, pp. 59–72; *Cat. of Coins in the Brit. Mus., Lesbos*, pl. XXXIX; Miss Patrick, pp. 73, 81; Jacoby, *Marmor Parium*, p. 101; Forrer, *Les Portraits de Sappho sur les monnaies*, in *Revue Belge de numismatique*, 1901, pp. 413 ff.; *Zeitschrift für Numismatik*, IX. 114, pl. IV.

106. *Meisterwerke*, p. 103.

107. *Greek Hero Cults and Ideas of Immortality*, Oxford, 1921, p. 367.

108. Walters, *Cat. of Terra-cottas in the British Museum*, London, 1903, pl. 19.

109. The ancient representations of Sappho on vases have been well studied by Jahn, *Darstellungen griechischer Dichter auf Vasenbildern*, Abh. d. Sächs. Ges. d. Wiss., VIII. 699 ff. (1861); Comparetti, *Museo Italiano di Antichita classica*, II, 41–80, pls. III–VI (1888); Cipollini, pp. 319–344; Wilamowitz, *Sappho und Simonides*, pp. 40 ff. Little new material has come to light, but the individual vases have been better interpreted in the later publications which we cite in other notes. Aly omits the busts, though he mentions the vases, but he calls the Steinhauser fragment a clay relief and fails to recognize that it is part of a vase.

110. Cf. Jahn, pl. III; Comparetti, *op. cit.*, pl. IV; Furt-wängler-Reichhold, *Gr. Vas.*, II, pp. 21 ff., 308 ff., pl. 64; Steiner, *Sappho*, pp. 54–5; Perrot et Chipiez, *Histoire de l'art*, X, p. 624, pl. 15; Beazley, *J. H. S.*, XLII, 1922, p. 91; Pfuhl, *Malerei und Zeichnung der Griechen*, Munich, 1923, p. 399;

Hoppin, *Handbook of Attic Red-figured Vases*, I, p. 461.
Hoppin wrongly rejects Furtwängler's attribution to the
factory of Brygus; and wrongly identifies Hauser's "Frau
Meisterin" with Beazley's Niobid Painter. Perrot (p. 626)
says that the Munich vase belongs to a contemporary of Duris
but that we shall never know the painter; but on p. 634 he
says: "we would be tempted to add the vase to the Berlin
amphora painter."

111. Comparetti, *op. cit.*, pl. III, 1; De Witte, *Antiq.
de l'hôtel Lambert*, no. 32, pl. III; Reinach, *Répertoire des Vases*,
I, p. 524. Formerly in the Dzialinsky collection at Paris.

112. Comparetti, *op. cit.*, pl. III, 2; Steiner, pp. 44 ff.;
Cipollini, p. 328; De Courten, p. III; Reinach *op. cit.*, I,
p. 525.

113. Comparetti, *op. cit.*, pl. V; Cipollini, p. 331; De
Courten, p. 95; *Röm. Mitt.* III, 1888, pl. IX; *Jahreshefte*,
VIII. 35–40 (1905); Nicole, *Meidias*, pl. VII; Reinach, *op. cit.*,
I, p. 526.

114. *B. C. H.*, IV. 373 (1880); Cipollini, pp. 337–8.

115. Cf. Comparetti, pl. VI; Steiner, pp. 16 ff.; Edmonds,
Class. Quart., XVI. 1 ff. (1922), where he fails to cite *Jahreshefte*, VIII. 40 (1905).

116. J. C. Hoppin, *Handbook of Attic Red-figured Vases*,
Harvard University Press, 1919, p. 410.

117. Murray, *White Athenian Vases in the British Museum*,
London, 1896, pl. XVII; Pfuhl, *op. cit.*, II, p. 546, fig. 527.

118. *Ann. d. Inst.*, XXX, 1858, p. 42, pl. B; Cipollini,
pp. 339–341.

119. Cf. Cipollini, pp. 343–4.

120. Cf. Nicole, *Meidias*, Geneva, 1908, pls. III and VI.
I cannot agree with Nicole in dating Meidias as late as 375–
350 B.C. He belongs to the time of the Peloponnesian War,
431–404 B.C. This fatal war did not stop the Athenians from
producing during war times such great works of art as the Erechtheum, beautiful vases and statues. Cf. also note 68 above.

121. Cf. Pfuhl, *op. cit.*, p. 566, III, Fig. 557; Pellegrini,
Museo Civico di Bologna, Catalogo dei Vasi Greci, pp. 133-135,
Fig. 77.

122. *N. H.*, XXXV. 141. Brunn, *Kunstgeschichte*, p. 299,

identifies him with a bronze-sculptor, Leon, but we are equally
ignorant about him.

123. *Anth. Plan.*, 310 (Edmonds, p. 173); Tatian, *Adv. Gr.*,
130.

124. Cf. Hermann, *Denkmäler der Malerei des Altertums*,
pl. 28; Pfuhl, *op. cit.*, p. 734; Lippold, *Röm. Mitt.*, XXXIII.
71 ff. (1918).

125. For replicas of the Sappho cf. Rizzo, *Rev. Arch.*, 1901,
pp. 301 ff. The latest and best discussion is by Percy Gardner,
J. H. S. XXXVIII. 10 ff. (1918). For a copy of Silanion's
Corinna at Compiègne cf. *Rev. Arch.* XXXII. 161 (1894) ;
XXXVI 169 (1898); Furtwängler, *Meisterwerke*, pp. 99 ff.
would class many of the so-called Sapphos as Aphrodite and
thinks that those which are copies of fifth century art may
represent the Aphrodite of Phidias which was to be seen in
later days in the portico of Octavia at Rome (Pliny, *N. H.*
XXXVI, 15).

126. II. 4. 57.

127. *Anth. Pal.*, VII. 15.

128. Cf. Fraenkel, *Inschriften von Pergamon*, 198. According to *C. I. G.* 3555 Jucundus and Cyriac of Ancona still
saw the inscription at Pergamum.

129. *Ecphr.*, 69–71.

130. On the Albani bust cf. *Jahrbuch*, V. 152 ff. (1890),
pl. III; Morcelli, Fea, Visconti, *Descr. della Villa Albani*,
1033; Schneider, *Jb. d. Ak. Kunstsammlungen*, XII, 72 ff.
(1891); Arndt, Brunn-Bruckmann, *Griechische und Römische Porträts*, pl. 147–148; for the bust in the Pitti cf.
Arndt, pls. 149–150; for that in the Uffizi, pls. 145–146; cf.
also Cipollini, pp. 345–356. On the Biscari and Naples busts cf.
Rizzo, *Rev. Arch.* XXXIX, 1901, pp. 301–307, pls. XXI, XXII.
On the Constantinople head cf. Mendel's *Cat.* no. 626.

131. *Art and Archaeology*, VI. 277 ff. (1917), Robinson,
ibid., pp. 285 ff. I have omitted mention of many other
ancient works of art wrongly supposed to represent Sappho,
such as Stackelberg, *Die Gräber der Hellenen*, Berlin, 1837,
pl. LXX, called Sappho with a female friend sitting in her
lap, merely because of the book-roll.

132. *Arch. Anzeiger*, XXVII. 124 (1912).

133. Cipollini, p. 405, pictures Magni's Saffo; p. 409 Confalonieri's Saffo; p. 413 Pradier's Sapho; p. 417 Pradier's standing Sapho; p. 421 Barrias' painting; p. 425 Gleyre's couch of Sappho. There is a bust of Sappho by Canova in Turin.

134. Cf. Reinach, in *Revue Archéologique*, XX, 2. 433-434 (1912), X, 2. 392 (1919).

135. Cf. for influence of Pamphos, a mythical poet earlier than Homer, Pausanias, IX. 29, 8; of Homer, *Neue Jahrbücher*, XXXIII 227 (1914); De Courten, pp. 74-76.

136. E. 114 influenced by *Theogony*, 3 ff.; E. 122 by *Works and Days*, 568; E. 81 by *Theogony*, 121.

137. Theognis, 1017.

138. Schol. Hesiod, *Works and Days*, 428.

139. Athenaeus, 554 b, 639 a.

140. Porphyrio on Horace, *Satires*, II. 1. 30, "ostendit Sapphonem et Alcaeum volumina sua loco sodalium habuisse."

141. Wilamowitz, *Textgeschichte der Bukoliker*, p. 88.

142. III. 153 f.; VI. 1181.

143. Wilamowitz, *Sappho und Simonides*, p. 58, 2. There is an enormous literature on Catullus' relation to Sappho and much discussion of textual matters. Cf. for the most recent *Bursian Jahresbericht*, CLXXVIII, 1919, p. 46. Compare E. 32, 147 and 149 with Catullus LXII, 26, 35; E. 151 with LXII, 61; E. 148 with LXII. In XXXV, 17-18 we have "Ignosco tibi, Sapphica puella Musa doctior."

144. *The Classical Quarterly*, XVI. 1-14 (1922).

145. IV. 9. 10.

146. II. 13. 24.

147. Cf. Ogle, *A. J. P.*, XLIII. 55 ff. (1922). For Sappho's influence on Horace cf. Pasquali, *Orazio lirico*, 1920. Most of the literature on the subject is not fit to read. Cf. Richard F. Burton's *The Book of the Thousand Nights and a Night*, Terminal Essay, X, p. 208, for a filthy, wrong interpretation of the word 'mascula'. It is surprising to find as great a modern scholar as Bloch, *Die Prostitution*, Berlin, 1912, I, p. 383, saying in his discussion of Homosexuality, ἀσέλγεια τριβακή, "Schon in früher Zeit galten Sparta und die Insel Lesbos als Orte, wo die weibweibliche Liebe be-

sonders verbreitet war und an letzterem Ort in der Dichterin Sappho eine weltberühmte Vertreterin fand." Cf. also on *tribadie* in Lesbos Bloch, *Der Ursprung der Syphilis*, II, pp. 586–588, where he thinks that he gives definite proof that Sappho was "eine echte Tribade." It is lamentable that as great a literary critic as J. A. Symonds should say that "Sappho gave this female passion an eminent place in Greek Literature; " see J. A. Symonds, *A Problem in Greek Ethics, An Inquiry into the Phenomenon of Sexual Inversion*, London, 1901, pp. 70–72. Fortunately the monograph was issued only in a very limited edition.

148. *Silvae*, V. 3. 154.

149. VII. 69.

150. *Symp.*, VII. 8. 2.

151. XIX. 9. 4.

152. *Loves*, 30.

153. *On Paid Companions*, 36; *Pictures*, 18.

154. On the influence of Sappho on Himerius cf. Rizzo, *Saggio su Imerio il sofista*, in *Riv. Fil. Cl.*, XXVI 513–16 (1898). In *Orations,* I. 4 the words τὸ λέχος Ὁμήρου were incomprehensible and Edmonds still omits Ὁμήρου, but the reading is undoubtedly correct and the significance is now apparent from the new epithalamium of Hector and Andromache.

155. XV. 35, 36, 37.

156. I. 16, 19, 20.

157. Cf. *Anth. Pal.*, V. 246; VII. 14, 15, 16, 17, 407, 718; IX. 26, 66, 184, 189, 190, 506, 521, 571; XVI. 310.

158. V. 246. I give a literal translation and Greek texts of all epigrams which mention Sappho in Miller-Robinson, *Songs of Sappho*.

159. Cf. *A. J. P.*, XXXVIII. 66 (1917).

160. Photius only cites the selections made by Sopater the Sophist, among which in his second book he included some quotations from Sappho's eighth book.

161. *Vita dell' Imperatore Alessio o Alesseide*, XV.

162. IV. 25.

163. His comment on Martial, VII. 67 is "Tribadem autem fuisse carmen indicat quod extat."

164. There is an interesting item in Natales Comes,

Mythologiae sive explicationes fabularum, Venice, 1551, Book V, c. XVI, p. 286, "Scriptum reliquit Sappho, Adonim mortuum fuisse a Venere inter lactucas depositum." According to Athenaeus 69 d, Cratinus had Aphrodite conceal Phaon among the "fair wild-lettuces."

165. In my library I have a copy dated 1696 of Anne Le Fèvre, *Les Poësies d'Anacréon et de Sapho*. This, however, is a second edition and the first was in 1681.

166. Welcker, *Kleine Schriften:* II, pp. 80 ff., *Sappho von einem herrschenden Vorurteil befreit*. Goethe occupied himself much with this article. For references in Goethe to Sappho cf. W. J. Keller, *Goethe's Estimate of the Greek and Latin Writers*, Madison, Wis., 1916, p. 51.

167. Sauer, *Grillparzer's sämtliche Werke*, Stuttgart, 1892, XIX, pp. 71 ff. For source of *Sappho* cf. *J. Engl. Germ. Phil.*, XXII, 503 ff. (1923).

168. Cf. Jean Giraud, *D'Après Sapho. Variations sur un thème éternel*, in *Revue d'Histoire littéraire de la France*, XXVII, 1920, pp. 194–203. I have added considerable material not there, since this article deals only with the second ode. I am indebted in this chapter to my learned colleagues, Professor Henry Carrington Lancaster and Professor Gilbert Chinard, for helpful suggestions.

169. *Traduction de quelques autres epigrammes Grecs*, *Œuvres de Ronsard*, Tome 2, Paris, 1889, p. 56.

170. The date is often wrongly given as 1682. In my copy, which is a second edition (Lyon 1696), it is stated that permission to publish the book was granted to Damoiselle Anne Le Fèvre on June 10, 1681, all rights to continue for six years. "Le dit livre a esté achevé d'imprimer pour la première fois le 1, Decembre 1681." My copy gives only the first two odes and the epigrams on Pelagon and Timas and quotes an inaccurate Latin prose translation of the first ode by her father. He has made several emendations, as in ode II, l. 7, ὡς βρόγχον, "nihil vocis pervenit ad fauces meas," as good a suggestion as Edmonds' creation of an unknown proper name Brocheo.

171. Cf. *Œuvres de Fontenelle* (Paris 1818), II, pp. 187, 188.

172. My copy is the thirteenth edition published by

Bertrand, Paris, 1818. The idea of a manuscript of Sappho found at Herculaneum is repeated by Lucy Milburn and Percy Mackaye.

173. My copy is dated London 1810 and is anonymous, *Poésies de Sapho suivies de différentes Poésies dans le même genre.* It contains also *Les Tourterelles de Zelmis* and the *Poésies Erotiques* of M. de Parny, who was such an admirer of Sappho. The adaptations are the same as those of Sauvigny. Why this edition is anonymous, I do not know.

174. XII, p. 181 ed. Furne, Jouvet et Cie., Paris.

175. My edition is Giguet et Michaud, Paris, 1805. This book with its long notes and citations, though little known, is important for the student of Sappho's influence.

176. Cf. Wilamowitz, *Sappho und Simonides,* pp. 63–69 on *Chansons de Bilitis,* pp. 71–78 on Lesbian Love.

177. Cf. Edwin M. Cox, p. 5, where he quotes Barnabe Barnes' *Parthenophil and Parthenophe,* 1593:

> *O, that I could make her, whom I love best,*
> *Find in a face, with misery wrinkled,*
> *Find in a heart, with sighs over ill-pined,*
> *Her cruel hatred.*

In Davison's *Poetical Rhapsody,* 1602, are some Sapphics by the mysterious "A. W." Here is a sample:

> *Hatred eternal, furious revenging,*
> *Merciless raging, bloody persecuting;*
> *Slanderous speeches, odious revilings;*
> *Causeless abhorring.*

In 1601 Campion and Roseter, *Lyrics, Elegies,* etc., give a clumsy example of Sapphic verse. In 1614 a tract called *The Martyrdom of Saint George of Cappadocia* contains at the end some "Sapphicks" which resemble the real Sappho only in having the same number of syllables to the verse. Cox and all others, so far as I know, fail to mention Sir Philip Sidney's translation of the second ode.

178. Cf. W. C. Lawton, *Sappho* with some new translations, *Lippincott Magazine,* 77, 583; W. A. R. Kerr, "*Sappho's Soliloquy,*" in *Canadian Magazine,* 12, 426; E. Saltus, "*Sappho,*" in *Lippincott's Magazine,* 51, 503; M. Thompson,

"*The Secret of Sappho*," in *The Atlantic Monthly*, 73, 365;
M. Gray, "*Sappho*," in *Argosy*, 51, 203; *Athenaeum*, 1889,
2, 56; F. B. Harte, "*Sappho of Green Springs*," in *Lippincott's
Magazine*, 45, 627; *Democratic Review*, 7, 18; Higginson, in
The Atlantic Monthly, 28, 83; G. Hill, in *Appleton's Journal*,
6, 158, 179; Mrs. Hamilton in *Harper's*, 56, 177 (has nothing
to do with the real Sappho); M. Thompson, "*Sappho's
Apple*," in *The Independent*, 53, 416; A. Chisholm, in *Canadian Magazine*, 15, 453; Reinach, *Révue Archéologique*, XXIV,
1914, 2, pp. 336–337; IX, 1919, p. 204; X, 1919, p. 225;
H. I. R., *Fragment of a Poem by Sappho done into English
verse*, in *The Literary Digest*, 48, 1493; "*Real Personal Character of the Poetess Sappho*," in *The Review of Reviews*, 46,
107–8; Swinburne, "*Sappho*," in *The Living Age*, 280, 817–
8; W. L. Courtney, "*Sappho and Aspasia*," in *The Fortnightly Review*, N.S. 91 (1912), 479–88; "*Sappho from the Dust*,"
in *The Literary Digest*, 48, 1362–3; M. M. Miller, "Sappho's
Songs of Exile," in *The Independent*, 87, 344; *New York
Nation*, 1914, 1, p. 602; Aldington, "*Letters to Unknown
Women*," in *The Dial*, 64, 430–1; W. A. Percy, *Sappho in
Leukas and Other Poems*, New Haven, 1915; Horton, "*New
Sappho Fragment in English Verse*," in *The Dial*, 61, 179;
Michael Monahan, "*Sappho*," in *All's Well or the Mirror Repolished*, II, 1922, pp. 87 ff.; Robinson, in *The Baltimore
Sun*, Jan. 22, 1922.

178a. In *Charmides* he says: "Or from the Lesbian
waters plucked drowned Sappho's golden quill."

179. See *Pericles and Aspasia*, Letters 47, 48, 82, 95, 149,
150, 152, 153.

180. *Idyls of the King, Lancelot and Elaine*, 1003–1004. Not
in Mustard, *Classical Echoes in Tennyson*, New York,
1904.

181. *Lyrics and Sonnets* (Edinburgh, 1903), p. 66.

182. Miller-Robinson, *Songs of Sappho*.

183. Litz, *Father Tabb*, Johns Hopkins Press, 1923, p.
168.

184. *Collected Poems*, New York, 1922, pp. 227–228.

185. *Art and Archaeology*, XII. 217 (1921).

NOTES

186. *Sappho in Leukas and other Poems*, Yale University Press, 1915.

187. *Art and Archaeology*, XV. 13 (1923).

188. J. U. Nicolson, *King of the Black Isles*, p. 3, Chicago, 1924.

SELECTED BIBLIOGRAPHY OF
RECENT BOOKS ON SAPPHO

ALY, see Pauly-Wissowa.

BASCOUL, J. M. F., *La chaste Sappho de Lesbos et le mouvement féministe à Athènes au IVe siècle av. J. C.* Paris. 1911.

BASCOUL, J. M. F., *La chaste Sappho de Lesbos et Stésichore. Les prétendues amies de Sappho.* Paris, 1913.

BERGK, TH., *Poetae Lyrici Graeci.* Vol. III, Leipzig, 1914.

BETHE, E., *Griechische Lyrik.* Berlin, 1920.

BRANDT, LIDA R., *Social Aspects of Greek Life in the Sixth Century B.C.* Philadelphia, 1921.

BRANDT, P., *Sappho, ein Lebensbild aus den Frühlingstagen altgriechischer Dichtung.* Leipzig, 1905.

BUNNER, ANNE, see Wharton.

CARMAN, BLISS, *Sappho, One Hundred Lyrics.* Boston, 1904.

CARROLL, M., *Greek Women.* Philadelphia, 1907.

CHRIST, W.VON-Schmid, W., *Geschichte der griechischen Litteratur.* Munich, 1912.

COX, E. M., *Sappho and the Sapphic Metre in English.* London, 1916. *Poems of Sappho.* London, New York, 1924.

CIPOLLINI, A., *Saffo.* Milan, 1890.

CROISET, A., *Histoire de la Litterature Grecque* (vol. II, pp. 226–244). Paris, 1898.

DE COURTEN, MARIA L. G., *Saffo* (Supplementi ad "Aegyptus"). Milan, 1921.

DIEHL, E., *Supplementum lyricum*[3] (Kleine Texte, 33–34). Bonn, 1917.

EDMONDS, J. M., *The New Fragments of Alcaeus, Sappho and Corinna.* Cambridge, 1909.

EDMONDS, J. M., *Sappho in the Added Light of the New Fragments.* Cambridge, 1912. (Has some poetical translations.)

EDMONDS, J. M., *Lyra Graeca*, I, in *The Loeb Classical Library*. New York, 1922. [Abbreviated as E.]

EDMONDS, J. M., Various articles in *Classical Review, Classical Quarterly* and *Cambridge Philological Society's Proceedings*, from 1909 to 1922.

FARNELL, G. S., *Greek Lyric Poetry*. London, 1891.

GLASER, R., *Sappho, die zehnte Muse* (Südwest-deutsche Monatsblätter). 1916.

GRENFELL, B. P., and HUNT, A. S., *The Oxyrhynchus Papyri*. Vols. I–XV, especially I, X, and XV. London, 1898. 1922.

HIGGINSON, T. W., *Atlantic Essays*. Boston, 1871.

LATINI, GIOV., *Saffo, Mimnermo e Catullo* Viterbo, 1914.

LAVAGNINI, B., *I Lirici Greci*. Turin, 1923.

LOBEL, E., *Sappho*. Oxford, 1925.

MACKAIL, J. W., *Lectures on Greek Poetry* (pp. 83–112). London and New York, 1911.

MEABE, T., *Saffo* (Spanish translation). Paris, 1913.

MERINO, A. FERNANDEZ, *Estudios de Literatura Griega. Safo ante la crítica moderna*.[3] Madrid, 1884.

MEUNIER, M., *Sappho, Traduction nouvelle de tous les fragments*. (Has not recent fragments.) Paris, 1911.

MILBURN, LUCY McD., *Lost Letters from Lesbos*. Chicago, 1902.

MILLER, MARION MILLS, and ROBINSON, D. M. *The Songs of Sappho* (Greek text of all Sappho, of all the epigrams about her, of Erinna, of the new papyrus biography of Sappho, etc., prepared and annotated and literally translated by D. M. Robinson. Introduction on *The Recovery and Restoration of the Egyptian Relics of Sappho* and a critical *Memoir of the Real Sappho* by D. M. Robinson. Introduction by M. M. Miller on the Sapphic Metre, and Poetical Adaptations of Sappho. New York, 1924.

MUSTARD, W. P., *Classical Echoes in Tennyson*. New York, 1904.

O'HARA, J. M., *The Poems of Sappho*. Portland, 1910.

OSBORN, PERCY, *Poems of Sappho*. London, 1909.

PASELLA, PIETRO, *I Frammenti di Alceo e di Saffo tradotti*. Rome, 1922.

[270]

PATRICK, MARY MILLS, *Sappho and the Island of Lesbos.* Boston, 1914. Reprinted, 1924.

PAULY-WISSOWA, – KROLL-WITTE, *Real-Encyclopädie.* Exhaustive article on Sappho by Aly. Stuttgart, 1920.

PETERSEN, W., *The Lyric Songs of the Greeks. Translated into English Verse.* Boston, 1918.

REINACH, TH., *Pour mieux connaître Sappho (Académie des Inscriptions et Belles-Lettres).* Paris, 1911.

ROBINSON, D. M. *See* Miller-Robinson.

SCOLLARD, C. L., – JONES, T. S., *Sapphics.* Clinton, N. Y., 1910.

SITZLER, J., *Bibliography on Sappho* in Bursian (Kroll) *Jahresbericht über die Fortschritte der klassischen Altertumswissenschaft.* CXXXIII, 1907, pp. 104 ff., pp. 176 ff., CLXXVIII, 1919, pp. 46 ff.

SMITH, J S. EASBY-, *Songs of Sappho.* Washington, D. C., 1891.

SMYTH, H. W., *Greek Melic Poets.* London, 1900.

STACPOOLE, H. D. V., *Sappho, a new rendering.* London 1920.

STANLEY, ALBERT A., *Greek Themes in Modern Musical Settings.* (Includes, pp. 1–68, Music to Percy Mackaye's *Sappho and Phaon*). *University of Michigan Humanistic Studies,* XV, 1923.

STEBBING, W., *Greek and Latin Anthology thought into English Verse.* Part III, *Greek Epigrams and Sappho.* Adaptations and Expansions of Sappho. None of the new fragments included. London, 1923.

STEINER, B., *Sappho.* Jena, 1907.

STORER, EDWARD, *Sappho (Poets Translation Series).* London, 1916.

TUCKER, T. G., *Sappho.* Melbourne, Australia, 1914.

TUTIN, J. R., *Sappho, The Queen of Song.* London and Boston, 1914.

VIVIEN, RENÉE [pseudonym of an American lady, Pauline Tarn, 1877–1909, who lived in Paris], *Sappho, traduction nouvelle avec le texte grec.* Paris, 1903. Reprinted in the anonymous *Sappho et huit poetesses grecques. Texte et reduction.* Paris, 1909.

WAGNER, R., *Übersetzung der grösseren Bruchstücke Sapphos im Versmass des Originals nebst erläuternden Bemerkungen.* 1916.

WALTHER, W., *Sappho aus dem Griechischen übersetzt*. Leipzig, 1914.

WAY, A. S., *Sappho and The Vigil of Venus*. London, 1920.

WAY, A. S., *Sappho*. London, 1923.

WHARTON, H. T., *Sappho, memoir, text, selected renderings* and a literal translation (with a collection also of poetic translations and paraphrases by various authors). First edition, London, 1885. Second edition, London and Chicago, 1887. Third edition, London, 1895. Fourth edition, 1898, and fifth edition, London, 1907. First edition without the revisions of later editions reprinted by Brentano, New York, in 1920, with metrical paraphrases of Sappho by Anne Bunner.

WILAMOWITZ-MÖLLENDORFF, ULRICH VON, *Textgeschichte der griechischen Lyriker*. Berlin, 1901.

WILAMOWITZ-MÖLLENDORFF und SCHUBART, *Berliner Klassikertexte*, Heft V. Berlin, 1907.

WILAMOWITZ-MÖLLENDORFF, ULRICH VON, *Sappho und Simonides* (with translations). Berlin, 1913.

WILAMOWITZ-MÖLLENDORFF, ULRICH VON, *Griechische Verskunst*. Berlin, 1921.

WRIGHT, F. A., *Feminism in Greek Literature from Homer to Aristotle*. New York, 1923.

KEY TO ILLUSTRATIONS

PLATE 2.   PITTACUS, LORD OF LESBUS

One of the seven wise men of Greece, in whose reign Sappho
was perhaps banished to Sicily. The bust was found in
Asia Minor in a Roman villa (100 A.D.). Formerly in Balti-
more in the collection of David M. Robinson, now in the
Museum of Budapest. Cf. *The Annual of the Budapest
Museum*, II, 1919–1920, p. 3. For other replicas cf. Lippold,
Griechische Porträt-Statuen, p. 72

PLATE 3. MYTILENE

Looking across the severing sea to Asia Minor

PLATE 4. THE STORY OF PHAON

From a fifth century hydria in Florence by the Meidias painter himself. Phaon, tired of the ladies' love-making, is seated in the middle below with the inscription "Phaon," over his head. Aphrodite is above in a chariot drawn by *Pothos* and *Himeros.* Reproduced from Milani, *Monumenti Scelti del R. Museo Archeologico di Firenze*, pl. III

PLATE 5. THE BEAUTIFUL PHAON

On a Greek vase in Palermo. Reproduced from Furtwaengler-Reichhold, *Griechische Vasenmalerei*, pl. 59

PLATE 6.   THE LEUCADIAN PROMONTORY

From an old engraving reproduced by Miss Patrick, *Sappho and the Island of Lesbos*, p. 96

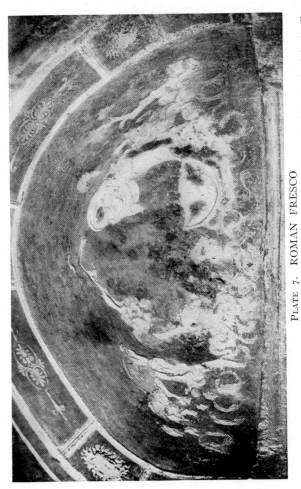

PLATE 7. ROMAN FRESCO

In an underground building found in Rome near the Porta Maggiore, showing to the left Apollo with lyre on the cliff, and to the right Sappho about to step off the rock into the sea, where a Triton waits with outspread garment. Behind Sappho higher up on the rock a winged Eros

PLATE 8. A PAPYRUS OF THE THIRD
CENTURY A.D.

With part of the text of a poem by Sappho. Reproduced
from *Oxyrhynchus Papyri*, XV, 1922, No. 1787, fragment
1, pl. II

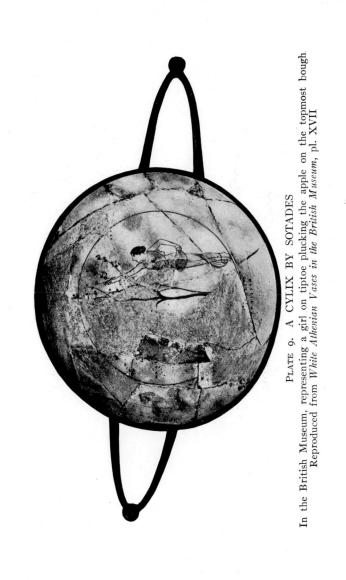

PLATE 9. A CYLIX BY SOTADES

In the British Museum, representing a girl on tiptoe plucking the apple on the topmost bough
Reproduced from *White Athenian Vases in the British Museum*, pl. XVII

PLATE 10. A GREEK COIN FROM MYTILENE
Showing probably Sappho's head on one side and
lyre on other. Enlarged twice the original size.
Reproduced from Miss Patrick, *Sappho and the
Island of Lesbos*, p. 73

PLATE 11. IMPERIAL COINS
In the British Museum, representing Sappho. Reproduced
from Miss Patrick, *op. cit.*, p. 81

PLATE 12. A GREEK VASE

In Munich, representing Alcaeus and Sappho. Reproduced from Furtwaengler-Reichhold, *op. cit.*, pl. 64

PLATE 13. A BLACK–FIGURED
CALPIS
Formerly in the Dzialinsky collection at Paris, now in Cracow, in
the style of the Nicoxenus painter,
with the earliest (about 500 B.C.)
inscribed representation of Sappho

PLATE 14. LOST LUCANIAN (?) VASE

Formerly in the Middleton collection. Sappho seated before a winged Eros who is bringing her a wreath. Reproduced from *Museo Italiano*, II, 1888, pl. III, 2

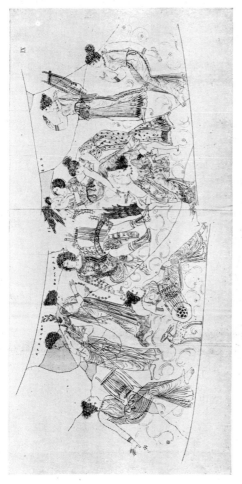

PLATE 15. GREEK ARYBALLUS

In the style of the Meidias painter, in the Jatta collection at Ruvo, representing Thamyris giving a musical recital in the presence of Apollo, Aphrodite, and the Muses, among whom Sappho is included. Reproduced from *Römische Mitteilungen*, III, 1888, pl. IX

PLATE 16. A FIFTH CENTURY GREEK HYDRIA

From Vari near Athens, showing Sappho seated and reading from a papyrus. According to Beazley the style is related to that of the Hector painter, though not by him. Reproduced from *Jahreshefte*, VIII, 1905, p. 40, Fig. 9

PLATE 17. PHAON ABOUT TO FERRY APHRODITE ACROSS THE SEA
On a Greek vase in Bologna. Reproduced from Pellegrini, *Catalogo dei Vasi Greci dipinti delle Necropoli Felsinee,* Fig. 77

PLATE 18. A POMPEIAN FRESCO
Supposed to represent Sappho and Alcaeus. Reproduced
from Herrmann-Bruckmann, *Denkmaeler der Malerei des
Altertums*, pl. 28

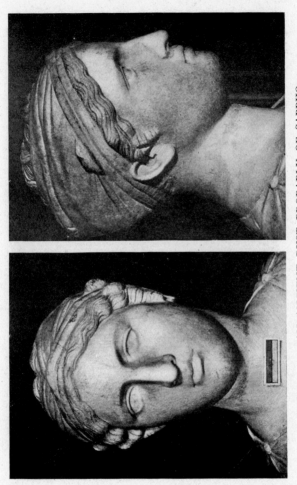

PLATE 19. AN ANCIENT BUST PROBABLY OF SAPPHO
In the Villa Albani, Rome. Reproduced from Arndt-Brunn-Bruckmann, *Griechische und Römische Porträts*, pls. 147–148

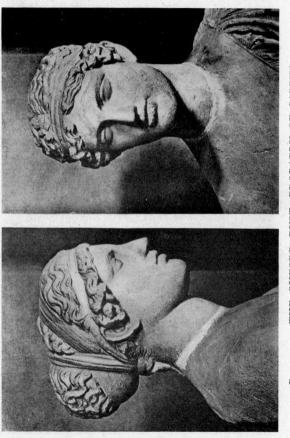

PLATE 20. THE OXFORD BUST, PROBABLY OF SAPPHO
Reproduced from *Journal of Hellenic Studies*, XXXVIII, 1918, pl. III

PLATE 21. BUST PROBABLY OF SAPPHO
In the Borghese Palace, Rome. Photographed in the
summer of 1922

PLATE 22. STATUE OF SAPPHO
By Magni

PLATE 23. A STATUE OF SAPPHO
By Pradier

PLATE 24. RAPHAEL'S PARNASSUS

In the Vatican. Sappho is leaning on the left side of the doorway

Our Debt to Greece and Rome

AUTHORS AND TITLES

AUTHORS AND TITLES

1. HOMER. John A. Scott, *Northwestern University*.
2. SAPPHO. David M. Robinson, *The Johns Hopkins University*.
3A. EURIPIDES. F. L. Lucas, *King's College, Cambridge*.
3B. AESCHYLUS AND SOPHOCLES. J. T. Sheppard, *King's College, Cambridge*.
4. ARISTOPHANES. Louis E. Lord, *Oberlin College*.
5. DEMOSTHENES. Charles D. Adams, *Dartmouth College*.
6. ARISTOTLE'S POETICS. Lane Cooper, *Cornell University*.
7. GREEK HISTORIANS. Alfred E. Zimmern, *University of Wales*.
8. LUCIAN. Francis G. Allinson, *Brown University*.
9. PLAUTUS AND TERENCE. Charles Knapp, *Barnard College, Columbia University*.
10A. CICERO. John C. Rolfe, *University of Pennsylvania*.
10B. CICERO AS PHILOSOPHER. Nelson G. McCrea, *Columbia University*.
11. CATULLUS. Karl P. Harrington, *Wesleyan University*.
12. LUCRETIUS AND EPICUREANISM. George Depue Hadzsits, *University of Pennsylvania*.
13. OVID. Edward K. Rand, *Harvard University*.
14. HORACE. Grant Showerman, *University of Wisconsin*.
15. VIRGIL. John William Mackail, *Balliol College, Oxford*.
16. SENECA. Richard Mott Gummere, *The William Penn Charter School*.
17. ROMAN HISTORIANS. G. Ferrero, *Florence*.
18. MARTIAL. Paul Nixon, *Bowdoin College*.
19. PLATONISM. Alfred Edward Taylor, *University of Edinburgh*.
20. ARISTOTELIANISM. John L. Stocks, *University of Manchester, Manchester*.
21. STOICISM. Robert Mark Wenley, *University of Michigan*.
22. LANGUAGE AND PHILOLOGY. Roland G. Kent, *University of Pennsylvania*.
23. RHETORIC AND LITERARY CRITICISM. (Greek) W. Rhys Roberts, *Leeds University*.
24. GREEK RELIGION. Walter W. Hyde, *University of Pennsylvania*.
25. ROMAN RELIGION. Gordon J. Laing, *University of Chicago*.

26. MYTHOLOGIES. Jane Ellen Harrison, *Newnham College, Cambridge.*
27. THEORIES REGARDING THE IMMORTALITY OF THE SOUL. Clifford H. Moore, *Harvard University.*
28. STAGE ANTIQUITIES. James T. Allen, *University of California.*
29. GREEK POLITICS. Ernest Barker, *King's College, University of London.*
30. ROMAN POLITICS. Frank Frost Abbott, *Princeton University.*
31. ROMAN LAW. Roscoe Pound, *Harvard Law School.*
32. ECONOMICS AND SOCIETY. M. T. Rostovtzeff, *Yale University.*
33. WARFARE BY LAND AND SEA. E. S. McCartney, *University of Michigan.*
34. THE GREEK FATHERS. Roy J. Deferrari, *The Catholic University of America.*
35. BIOLOGY AND MEDICINE. Henry Osborn Taylor, *New York.*
36. MATHEMATICS. David Eugene Smith, *Teachers College, Columbia University.*
37. LOVE OF NATURE. H. R. Fairclough, *Leland Stanford Junior University.*
38. ASTRONOMY AND ASTROLOGY. Franz Cumont, *Brussels.*
39. THE FINE ARTS. Arthur Fairbanks, *Museum of Fine Arts, Boston.*
40. ARCHITECTURE. Alfred M. Brooks, *Swarthmore College.*
41. ENGINEERING. Alexander P. Gest, *Philadelphia.*
42. GREEK PRIVATE LIFE, ITS SURVIVALS. Charles Burton Gulick, *Harvard University.*
43. ROMAN PRIVATE LIFE, ITS SURVIVALS. Walton B. Mc-Daniel, *University of Pennsylvania.*
44. FOLK LORE.

45. GREEK AND ROMAN EDUCATION.

46. CHRISTIAN LATIN WRITERS. Andrew F. West, *Princeton University.*
47. ROMAN POETRY AND ITS INFLUENCE UPON EUROPEAN CULTURE. Paul Shorey, *University of Chicago.*
48. PSYCHOLOGY.
49. MUSIC. Théodore Reinach, *Paris.*
50. ANCIENT AND MODERN ROME. Rodolfo Lanciani, *Rome.*